Ryumeikan surpasses the bounds of time.

龍名館、時を越える

ホテル龍名館お茶の水本店

目次

はじめに ... 6

ごあいさつ
　四代目当主　代表取締役会長　浜田章男 ... 8
　五代目当主　代表取締役社長　浜田敏男 ... 10

第一章　ホテル龍名館お茶の水本店　次世代ホテルへの挑戦 ... 12
　古き懐かしき時代から新しい鼓動の誕生へ ... 14
　受け継ぐ真髄と斬新なものとの調和 ... 18
　たった九室だからできること ... 22
　お客さまとともに和の心、おもてなしの心で ... 24
　思い　支配人　和賀茂樹 ... 26

第二章　ようこそ、ホテル龍名館お茶の水本店へ ... 28
　語る　アーティスト　ミヤケマイ氏 ... 44
　語る　プロデューサー　芹沢高志氏 ... 48

第三章　ホテル龍名館お茶の水本店　客室のご案内 ... 52
　語る　信楽焼き陶器浴槽　丸元製陶

Table of Contents

Prologue　6

Message from Akio Hamada, the fourth-generation
hotel representative and Chairman　8

Message from Toshio Hamada, the fifth-generation
hotel representative and President　10

Chapter 1:
Challenge of Transforming Hotel Ryumeikan
Ochanomizu Honten into a Next-Generation Hotel　12

From good old days to the birth of a new heart　14

Harmony between the essence of tradition and novel design　18

The potential of nine guest rooms　22

Sharing wholehearted Japanese hospitality with guests　24

General manager Shigeki Waga　26

Chapter 2:
Welcome to Hotel Ryumeikan Ochanomizu Honten　28

Designer Mai Miyake　44

Interview with Producer Takashi Serizawa　48

Chapter 3:
A Guide to the Guest Rooms of
Hotel Ryumeikan Ochanomizu Honten　52

Interview with Ikuo Muraki,
President of Marumoto Seitoh,
a manufacturer of Shigarakiyaki(ceramic) bathtubs　64

Arichika Iwata, President of Iwata Inc.,
a bed mattress manufacturer　68

Art Director Takashi Taira of Ideal Design & Product　78

Chapter 4:
Aiming to offer "dining and tea steeped with hospitality"　82

Interview with Executive Chef Masafumi Okubo　92

Closing words　98

第四章　「お茶のあるおもてなしの食風景」を目指して　82

思い　料理長　大久保将史　92

おわりに　98

代表取締役　村木郁夫氏　64

語る　ベッド（マットレス）イワタ
代表取締役社長　岩田有史氏　68

語る　アートディレクター
イデアルデザインアンドプロダクト　大良隆司氏　78

はじめに

地方創生が国家レベルの課題として謳われているものの、東京は首都圏集中型の状況となっています。東京都の人口は一三〇〇万人を超え、昼間人口は一五〇〇万人に達しています。就業人口は八〇〇万人強、まさに首都圏一極集中化が進み今もなお人口が増え続けています。

そんな中、「神田・お茶の水」に創業百十余年、悠久の昔からひっそりと時を刻んでいるホテルがあります。それが「ホテル龍名館お茶の水本店」です。大正十二年の関東大震災、そして昭和十四年に火ぶたが切られた第二次世界大戦。天災そして戦争という人災により日本国の中枢であった東京は火災と空襲により火の海と化しました。多くの人命を失いました。関東大震災のとき、ホテルは周囲に建物の少ない、閑静な場所にあったことから焼失は免れると思っていましたが、思いむなしく焼失してしまいました。何とか再建をはたしたものの、第二次世界大戦にともなう東京大空襲に見舞われたのです。このとき、本店だけは焼けることなく終戦を迎えました。

――万緑の槐百年の店守る――　孝子（三代目の妻）

本店の敷地内には、創業時からこの地に根を下ろす槐（えんじゅ）の木が、どんな状況下でも新芽をつけてくれました。関東大震災の火災で焼けこげたものの、苦しい人々のために尽くしてきた宿、店主を守り、そして人々に生きることのたくましさを、生き抜くための自らの生命力を持って教え続け、勇気を与えてくれていたのです。そんな歴史を刻んできた龍名館が新たな百年を刻み続けていくために平成二十六年夏、新たな一歩を踏み出したのです。しかも、これからの世代を生きる二十代、三十代のスタッフの若い力を結集し、街の旅館の系譜を継ぐ次世代ホテルとして、そして神田・お茶の水のブランドホテルとして――。さらにお茶の水でもない、神田でもない、閑静な神田駿河台交差点を核とした街の中の街のホテルとして――。いや、旅館として立ち上がったのです。本書は平成二十六年夏、ビルの中にある二フロア、九室という小さなホテルの改装にいたった経緯、そして経営者とスタッフの「ホテル龍名館お茶の水本店」への熱い思いを凝縮させた一冊です。

Prologue

Regional revitalization is a major issue facing Japan today. However, everything is concentrated in the Tokyo Metropolitan district, and the population of Tokyo continues to increase. There are more than 13 million people living in Tokyo, with a working population a little over 8 million, and in the daytime the population surpasses 15 million. As these figures show, there is a large concentration of people and businesses in and around Tokyo. In the midst of this hustle and bustle, the Hotel Ryumeikan Ochanomizu Honten has stood quietly in the Kanda-Ochanomizu area since it was first established more than 110 years ago. Large sections of Tokyo were burned and devastated by the fires resulting from the Great Kanto Earthquake of 1923 and the airstrikes during World War II, which broke out in 1939. These natural and man-made disasters claimed many lives. When the Great Kanto Earthquake struck Tokyo, the hotel was located in a quiet place with only a few buildings in the surrounding neighborhood. For this reason, we initially believed that the hotel would escape the flames, but unfortunately it was ultimately burned to the ground. We managed to reconstruct the hotel, but it was struck by the Great Tokyo Air Raid of March 10, 1945 towards the end of World War II. Only the head building survived the fires that swept across the city.

The enju tree with its myriad green leaves has protected our hotel for 100 years—Takako(wife of the third-generation proprietor)

The enju tree (pagoda tree) standing on the grounds of the head building has always produced new buds since the days the hotel was first founded, no matter how difficult the times may be. Even though the tree suffered fire damage during the Great Kanto Earthquake, it continues to watch over the hotel and its keeper who have devoted themselves to helping struggling people, and encourages them with its vitality by producing new buds.

The Hotel Ryumeikan story has been an eventful one, and in the summer of 2014 the hotel took a new step forward in the chapter for the next 100 years ahead. The Hotel Ryumeikan fully draws upon the power of young staff in their twenties and thirties who will play an active part in years to come, and has risen anew as a next-generation hotel carrying on the tradition of inns in the town. It has established itself both as a brand in the Kanda-Ochanomizu area and as a hotel committed to developing a town organized around the intersection of Kanda Surugadai, a quiet district that survived the fires of the Great Kanto Earthquake and World War II. This book is the culmination of our efforts to explain why we transformed the hotel in the summer of 2014 into a small establishment with two floors and nine rooms housed in a single building, and convey the fervent passion the hotel head and staff have for the Hotel Ryumeikan Ochanomizu Honten.

母が書き残した三つの言葉を忘れず、さらなる成長を

四代目当主 代表取締役会長 浜田章男 ごあいさつ

和風旅館であった―。
なまけてはいけない―。
龍名館の看板に（頭を下げる）―。

母直筆の文書に書き残されていた"忘れてはいけないこと"の三つです。まさにこの三つの言葉が明治三十二年の始まり以来、龍名館が守り続けている家訓でもあります。

私の父、浜田隆は昭和二十三年三代目当主として迎え入れられ、まさに日本の高度成長の中、生き抜いてきました。慣れ親しんだ本店を高層ビルに建て替えたのですが、父も母も本当にそれで良いのかと迷っている姿をよく目にした記憶があります。しかし、戦後の日本の経済成長は目まぐるしいほど発展を遂げ、周囲には高層ビルが建ち、戦中、戦後を生き抜いてきた旅館も老朽化が進みま

Never forget the three lessons for future growth that my mother left us

Message from Akio Hamada, the fourth-generation hotel representative and Chairman

Never forget our roots as a Japanese-style inn (ryokan)
Never be idle
Always show guests the deep respect befitting the name *Ryumeikan*

The words above are three lessons my mother penned in a notebook regarding the things we must always keep in mind. Ryumeikan has been committed to these three principles since its establishment in 1899. My father, Takashi Hamada, was welcomed as the third-generation head in 1948 and guided the hotel through the period of Japan's high-speed economic growth. My father and mother decided to rebuild the familiar head building into a high rise, but I remember well their reluctance to make this decision. The economic growth of postwar Japan was tremendous. High-rise buildings were built around our hotel, and many inns that had survived the war and the early years of the postwar period fell by the wayside. In addition, the Tokyo Olympics in 1964 triggered a rush to build modern hotels. Watching these developments unfold, we found ourselves standing at a crossroads as an accommodation establishment. In the spring of 1975, we built a new head building that also contained a business office. I became the fourth-generation head in 1995, and embarked on a plan to rebuild Yaesu Ryumeikan. In 2005, my younger brother became the fifth-generation proprietor and put the plan into action. The hotel was renamed the Hotel Ryumeikan Tokyo in June 2009. To be honest, I did not agree with the recent renovation of the head building. Our hotel was originally a Japanese ryokan with twelve rooms, and I wondered about the reasons for reducing the number of rooms to nine in terms of hotel management. However, the baton is now being passed on to the next generation, and I greatly respect their way of thinking and passion. I hope the young generation will continue to honor the brand and value, or more specifically the prestige that has been passed down for more than 110 years, and protect Ryumeikan through the addition of new brands so that it will always be cherished. I also sincerely hope that Ryumeikan will be a hotel that plays a significant role in developing the Kanda-Ochanomizu community, working in cooperation with the Surugadai neighborhood association made up of fifty to sixty hotel members, a local shrine festival held every other year, and stores in the neighborhood. We will never be idle in our work, but approach it with modesty and earnest attention to the spirit of Japanese-style inns. Ryumeikan is a unique hotel managed by three generations of keepers: the fourth... the fourth, fifth, and sixth. I graciously ask for your continued support as we work to write the next chapter of the Ryumeikan story.

一流ブランドに
飽きて
しまった方の
第二の故郷に

五代目当主　代表取締役社長　浜田敏男　ごあいさつ

四代目当主の兄より引き継ぎ五代目当主として平成二十一年より就任いたしました。とにかく両親に教えられてきたのは〝お客さまのために尽くすこと〟です。この商売ですからあたりまえのように聞こえますが、本当にお客さまと向き合い、お客さまが求めていることを徹底的に行なうことは難しいことです。中には理不尽なこともあります。そんなときはよく母が言っていた〝龍名館の看板に頭を下げる〟という言葉を思い出します。自分では納得がいかず頭を下げたくなくても、龍名館と言う看板を背負っていること、そしてその看板に対して頭を下げると思えば、どんな理不尽なことでも寛容に受け入れることができます。また龍名館は小さいからこそ常に走りながら考え、問題解決しています。立ち止まって考えていたらすべてが止まってしまいます。改善すべきことが見つかったとき、気づいたときにどうすればよいのかを考え、判断し実行することを常に繰り返しています。どんなものにも完璧なことはなく、時代の流れとともに求められるハード、

Seeking to be loved as a second home by those who have had enough of first-class brands

Message from Toshio Hamada, the fifth-generation hotel representative and President

I took over as President and the fifth-generation hotel head in 2009, succeeding my older brother, the fourth-generation representative. My parents taught me the importance of "wholehearted devotion to guests." This may sound quite natural for this line of business, but it is really difficult to honestly consider and fully respond to customer needs. Sometimes I find customer demands to be outrageous. But when confronted with these situations, I remember one of my mother's lessons: "Always show guests the deep respect befitting the name Ryumeikan." Even if I feel uncomfortable about something and reluctant to extend this respect, I can tolerate the unreasonable by remembering that I represent Ryumeikan, and afford the hotel the respect worthy of the name. In addition, because Ryumeikan is a small hotel, it is always on the move and thinking of ways to solve problems. If we think stopping, everything will come to a stop. When we find something that can be improved, we think about how to address the situation, make a decision, and take action. This is a cycle we constantly repeat.

In this world, nothing is perfect. The required hardware, software, and means for conveying information change with the passage of time. Despite these changes, we maintain the enduring essence of Ryumeikan, and that is something we will never change. However, if change proves to be the only way we can achieve success in business, we should move forward with reforms while the potential extent of damage is small. The Hotel Ryumeikan Tokyo, which opened at the Yaesu entrance of Tokyo Station in 2009, was affected by the Great East Japan Earthquake of 2011. In addition, the competitive appeal of some of our guest rooms declined due to the change of the environment surrounding the hotel. In response to this situation, we thought hard about how to prevent our guest rooms from losing their competitive edge while at the same time enhancing their appeal, and quickly implemented measures that focused on delivering a "comfortable sleeping experience." Thanks to these measures, occupancy rates gradually rose, and the Hotel Ryumeikan Tokyo also gained greater publicity. Now our establishment is held in high regard by a broad range of customers. I should say that our recent renewal was something of an adventure. We considered a plan for an accommodation-focused hotel and outsourcing or franchising the restaurant business. However, we returned to the fact that we were originally a Japanese ryokan, and concluded that our efforts to preserve the head building as our flagship hotel for the next generation were essential in terms of both internal and external factors, and that they would give rise to new brands.

I hope people will continue to look on Ryumeikan as a second home and an alternative to first-class brands. In turn, we will continue to sincerely and wholeheartedly welcome guests to ensure our hotel is loved for years to come.

そしてソフトや、情報の発信方法は変わります。もちろん連綿と続く龍名館たるべき真髄は変えません。変えてはいけません。しかしながら、変えなくてはうまくいかないのであれば傷が浅いうちに改革をすべきです。平成二十一年に開業した東京駅八重洲口の「ホテル龍名館東京」も平成二十三年に起きた東日本大震災の影響を受けました。またホテルの周囲の環境の変化により一部の客室の商品力が落ちてしまう問題も起きました。しかしその中で、どうしたら商品力を落とさず、むしろ上げていくことができるのかを考え、いち早く「快眠」をテーマにテコ入れしたのです。すると徐々に稼働率は上がり、ホテル龍名館東京の知名度も高まり、今ではさまざまなところから評価をいただいております。今回のリニューアルもある意味、冒険ではありません。宿泊特化型のホテル構想や飲食店の外部委託やFC展開なども検討しましたが、やはり元々、旅館であった姿を本店、つまりフラッグシップホテルとして次世代に伝えていくことが、社内的にも社外的にも不可欠であり、それが新たなブランドを作り出すのだという結論に達した次第です。一流ブランドに飽きてしまったお客さまの第二の故郷として、これからも龍名館をご支持いただき、そしていつまでも愛されるホテルとしてスタッフ一同、誠心誠意を込めてお迎えいたします。

第一章 ホテル龍名館お茶の水本店 次世代ホテルへの挑戦

ホテル龍名館お茶の水本店のリニューアルにあたり、若手スタッフの間で、"これまでの百年も、そしてこれからの百年も神田・お茶の水のブランドホテルとして愛される龍名館であり続けたい"という願いを、どのように表現し、空間、モノとして具現化できるのか―。をテーマに開業二年前、平成二十四年より私達の挑戦が始まりました。

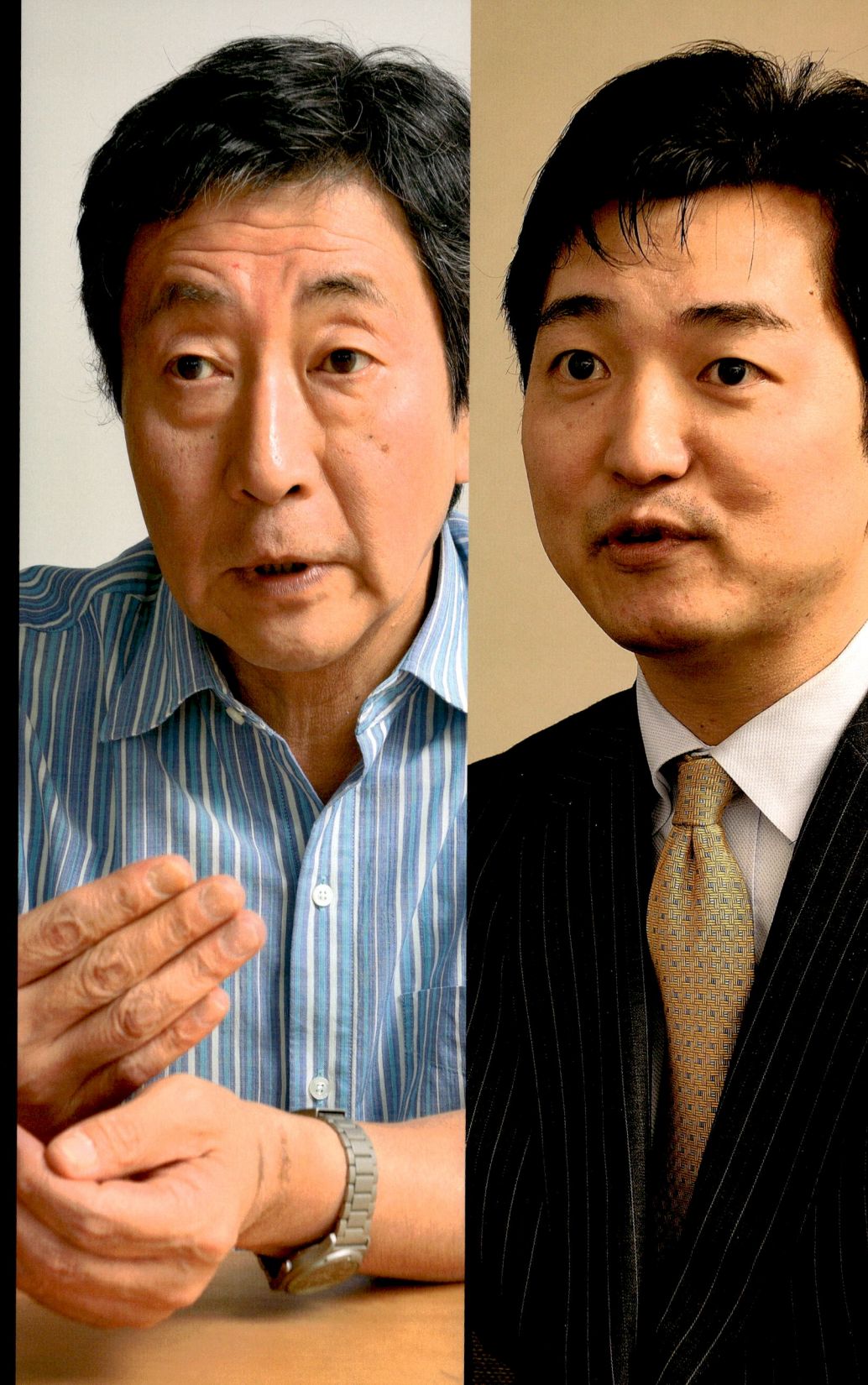

Chapter 1: Challenge of Transforming Hotel Ryumeikan Ochanomizu Honten into a Next-Generation Hotel

In renewing the Hotel Ryumeikan Ochanomizu Honten, the young staff discussed how to express their passion for "a 100-year old brand hotel in the Kanda-Ochanomizu area that will remain cherished for the next 100 years," and how to add substance to this passion in the form of space and tangible things. These discussions gave rise to a new challenge in 2012, two years before the renovation.

古き懐かしき
時代から
新しい鼓動の
誕生へ

From good old days
to the birth
of a new heart

The history of Ryumeikan dates back to 1899, when it was established by Uhei Hamada in Kogachou in Kanda, Tokyo (current Kanda Surugadai). Uhei was the fourth-generation head of a branch family of the Nagura-ya Ryokan, which had been in business in the Nihonbashi Muromachi area of Tokyo since the Edo period. The name "Ryumeikan" was taken from the name of Uhei's older sister, "*tatsu* (dragon)," and "*na* (name)" of Nagura-ya. The inn was a two-story building, and all the rooms faced a garden. The sophisticated Japanese-style design fascinated persons of good taste and famous people from many different fields, earning the hotel coverage by different magazines of that time. The Hamada family also paid special attention to the furnishings and selected a number of unique items. The first-generation inn head Uhei, who was a collector of new and novel things, built a Western-style restaurant in a section of the garden and hired a full-time cook to serve Western cooking. His wife Uta also had a keen eye for business, and together their hotel business made smooth progress. Business did so well they were able to open branch hotels in Gofukubashi and Sarugakucho at the beginning of the Taisho era. In 1918, Jiro Hamada (original name, Jiro Takaku) took over as the second-generation head. However, five years later the Great Kanto Earthquake struck Tokyo in 1923. The fires caused by the massive earthquake were much more powerful than he anticipated, and all three of his stores—the head building and two branches—were burned to ashes. In this desperate situation, he needed a large amount of funding to rebuild the family business. He requested Mr. Honma, an esteemed hotel guest who lived in Sakata, Yamagata, for financial support. Mr. Honma responded to Jiro's request and generously provided financial support at no interest and without a fixed period for repayment. Jiro built a new two-story inn with eight rooms in preparation for the Olympics scheduled to be held in Tokyo in 1940. However, the dark clouds of war began to enshroud Japan in the late 1930s, and the Olympics were ultimately cancelled. Shortly thereafter World War II began in 1939. In the fall of 1944, Jiro began to rent the new inn and hall to the Ministry of Greater East Asia, but by that time the war was already steadily growing worse. In the spring of 1945 the Gofukubashi branch, the Nagura-ya Ryokan, and the Chiyoda Ryokan (closely associated with Ryumeikan) were all completely destroyed by air raids. The head inn, which managed to survive the air raids, was opened for use as accommodation for people who had lost their homes, family, and friends during the bombings.

龍名館の歴史は明治三十二年までさかのぼります。その年、東京・日本橋室町で江戸時代から営業していた「名倉屋旅館」の分家として四代目を継ぐ濱田卯平衛が、東京・神田区甲賀町（現・神田駿河台）に龍名館を創業しました。龍名館という名は姉の名前「辰」と名倉屋の「名」にちなんだものです。建物は総二階建てで、部屋はすべて庭に面していました。洗練された和風の造りは趣味人や各界の人々を惹きつけ、当時の雑誌にも紹介されるほどだったようです。什器備品にもこだわり、選び抜かれた品々を使っていました。新しいもの好きだった初代は、庭の一画に西洋館を造り、コックを常駐させ洋食も振る舞いました。妻・うたも事業熱心だったことから、旅館経営は順調に軌道に乗り、大正時代のはじめには、呉服橋支店、猿楽町分店を出店するほどに発展を遂げました。大正七年、濱田次郎（旧姓・高久次郎）が二代目として当主を継ぎました。ところが、大正十二年、関東大震災が起きました。火の勢いは予想を上回り、本店、支店、分店の三店舗ともすべてが焼失しました。そのため、多額の再建資金が必要でしたが、お客さまの一人であった山形県・酒田の本間氏に資金援助のお願いをしたところ、無利息、無期限で資金援助の承諾を得ることができたのです。オリンピックが日本で開催されることとなり、二階建て八室の新館を建築しました。ところが戦争の色が濃くなりオリンピックの開催は中止、さらに戦争が始まったのです。昭和十九年の秋からは、本店の新館は広間も含めて「大東亜省」の官舎としてお貸しすることとなりました。しかし戦況はますます悪化し、昭和二十年春、呉服橋支店、名倉屋旅館、千代田旅館（龍名館と関係の深い旅館）ともに空襲でで焼失いたしました。空襲の被害を免れた本店は親戚・知人はもちろんのこと、焼け出された人々の宿泊場所として開放したのです。

ホテル龍名館東京 ロビー

After the war ended, the first thing we did was to rebuild the Gofukubashi branch. Takashi Hamada (original name, Takashi Nomoto), took over as the third-generation head in 1948 after the new small inn was completed. Years passed and in 1973, right when Japan was in the middle of a period of rapid economic growth, the third-generation head made a decision to rebuild the old head inn we had long used as a high-rise building. In the years that followed, we took on new businesses, including the opening of the Japanese restaurant "Hanagoyomi" in Roppongi. Akio Hamada was appointed as the fourth-generation head in 1995. He was passionate about pursuing a new approach for injecting our inherited tradition and sincerity into business, and embarked on a plan to rebuild the Hotel Yaesu Ryumeikan. Toshio Hamada, the fifth-generation head and Akio's younger brother, took over the project and opened the Hotel Ryumeikan Tokyo in June 2009. The hotel was highly regarded for its warm inn-like hospitality and good team work of the cooperative staff. It appeared in rankings on various tourist websites, and was also introduced in travel guides and many other kinds of books. Now, we are working to renovate our head building, which represents the essence of Ryumeikan. This building survived the Great Kanto Earthquake and World War II under the protection of an enju tree (pagoda tree) that has continued to give people courage and hope. We needed to create a new heart to channel the blood running through Ryumeikan for more than 110 years into the next generation, one that would not be rejected, but beat more smoothly and strongly than ever before. For this project, we organized a team led by Hiroaki Hamada, who is in line to be the sixth-generation head, and first sought to establish the concept that would form the basis of this project. In this process, we reconsidered and discussed the positioning, survival strategy, and presence of Ryumeikan from many different points of view. This new heart has started beating.

戦後――、まずは呉服橋支店の再建に着手しました。ささやかながらも、その実現ができたころ、三代目を継ぐ人物として昭和二十三年、浜田隆（旧姓・野本隆）を迎え入れました。時代は移り変わり、昭和四十八年、日本はまさに高度成長のさなかにありました。三代目は意を決し、慣れ親しんできた本店を高層ビルに建て替える決断をしたのです。その後は和食会席「花ごよみ」を六本木に出店するなど、昭和から平成にかけて新規事業にも取り組みました。平成七年、四代目当主に浜田章男が就任しました。受け継いだ伝統と真心を、さらに新鮮な視点から事業に活かしていきたいと考え、ホテル八重洲龍名館建替計画を開始。その意志を弟の浜田敏男（五代目）が受け継ぎ、平成二十一年六月、「ホテル龍名館東京」を開業しました。旅館を思わせる温かなおもてなしや、スタッフ間のチームワークの良さはさまざまな旅行サイトのランキングで評価され、またガイドブックを始めとする多くの書籍にも掲載されました。そして今――、関東大震災、第二次世界大戦を生き抜いてきた龍名館の真髄である本店の改装に、勇気と希望を与え続けられた槐の木に見守られ、着手しました。百十余年生き続けてきた龍名館に連綿と流れている血をきちんとなめらかに――そしてこれまで以上にたくましく鼓動する心臓です。このプロジェクトは将来的に六代目当主となる濱田裕章を中心にチームを編成し、まずは根幹となる構想作りに着手しました。そのために改めて龍名館の在り方、生き方、存在意義について、さまざまな角度から議論を重ねていきました。まさに新たな心臓として鼓動を打ち始めたのです。

受け継ぐ真髄と斬新なものとの調和

古来より受け継がれてきた日本の住空間、そしてそこで育まれてきた和の心のありようを多くの人に感じていただきたい。そんな切なる想いから、スタッフ一人ひとりが旅と宿のスタイルを見立てて、そこに訪れるお客さまとともに「ホテル龍名館お茶の水本店」を創っていきます。創業百十余年の変遷の中で変わらない真髄です。

多くの文化人に愛された龍名館
一九五五年（昭和三〇）、幸田露伴の次女で小説家の幸田文氏が、小説『流れる』にて帝国ホテルに並ぶ名店だと称したほか、伊東深水や川村曼舟ら、画家や多くの文化人に愛されてきました。第二次世界大戦中には委任統治領、占有地域の統治を行なう「大東亜省」の官舎として本店の新館全室と広間を提供していました。
そして二〇一五年（平成二七）、戦後七〇年。激動の時代を乗り越えながら時代に寄り添うようにこの地で生き抜いてきました。まさに神田・お茶の水を代表する旅館であったのです。

Harmony between the essence of tradition and novel design

Hotel Ryumeikan Ochanomizu Honten desires to provide as many people as possible with the opportunity to experience the Japanese residential space that has been passed down since the days of yore, along with the sense of Japanese hospitality that has been nurtured by this space. The Ryumeikan staff members embody this passion, and are committed to supporting our hotel together with guests, paying special attention to their means of travel and accommodation. This approach is the core essence of our hotel, and it has remained constant in the face of ceaseless change for the 110 years since we were first established.

Ryumeikan was loved by many intellectuals. In 1955, novelist Aya Kouda, the second daughter of Rohan Kouda, hailed Ryumeikan as a fine inn comparable to the Imperial Hotel in her novel. Many painters, including Shinsui Ito and Manshu Kawamura, also loved our hotel. During World War II, we offered all the rooms and the hall of the head inn to the Ministry of Greater East Asia, which governed countries under its jurisdiction and occupied regions. We are now in 2015, the 70th anniversary of the end of World War II. We survived the maelstrom of each age, and to this day stand as a hotel synonymous with the Kanda-Ochanomizu area.

「街の旅館」という自負

旅館におけるホテルとは異なります。お客さまと一定の距離を保ちながらも相手の懐に入る人肌に触れるサービスです。まさに街の旅館としてスタートしたのです。どんなときもお客さまのために誠心誠意を尽くしてきました。お客さまには最高のお部屋を提供したいという思いから、「家族・従業員は旅館の中で最も陽の当たらない場所に住むように」と先代から伝えられています。画家などの文化人からは、いくらの値がつくか分からない絵画を宿泊代の代わりに受け取ったこともあったそうです。また理不尽なことを言うお客さまに対しても頭を下げました。それは街の旅館「龍名館」という看板を背負っていることを常に念頭においていたからです。

斬新さへの探求

旧名倉屋旅館では日本ではまだ珍しかったエレベーターの導入、龍名館では西洋料理の提供を行っていました。さらに客室には洋間も取り入れ、この試みは龍名館が初めてだったと言われています。

「神田・お茶の水」

龍名館は閑静な神田駿河台に建っています。最寄駅はJR御茶ノ水駅。近くには書店や古本屋が立ち並ぶ神田神保町、そして少し東に進めば電気街が有名であり、最近ではサブカルチャーの発信地としても人気のある秋葉原、お茶の水方面に進むとニコライ堂や神田明神があり、銀座やレンガ造りを復刻させた東京駅にもとても近い距離にあります。さまざまな名所や人気スポットが入りまじったエリアです。

Pride in being a "town inn"

The Okami (landlady) and nakai (waitress) working in a Japanese-ryokan are different from hoteliers and hotel attendants. Although inns maintain a certain distance in their relationship with guests, they make sure to provide them with heartfelt services. We began as a town inn, and we have always offered wholehearted services to guests. The first-generation head, who had a keen passion for providing guests with the best rooms, often said that "the family and employees of the inn stay in the spot that gets the least sunshine." There have been instances when painters and other people of culture have given us priceless creations in exchange for lodging fees. Though there are times we receive outrageous requests from guests, we always remain focused on presenting a good image of Ryumeikan as a town inn.

Quest for novelty

The old Nagura-ya Ryokan installed an elevator at a time when elevators were still quite rare in Japan, while Ryumeikan served Western cuisine. We also introduced Western-style guest rooms, and this attempt was said to be the first of its kind in the hotel industry in Japan.

The Kanda-Ochanomizu area

Ryumeikan is located in Kanda Surugadai, a quiet area. The nearest station is JR Ochanomizu Station close to the Kanda Jimbocho area, famous for its splendid array of secondhand book stores that line the streets. A little to the east is Akihabara, which was once famous for being a major home electric appliance shopping district, but in recent years it has become known as a popular subculture center. Towards JR Ochanomizu Station, you can enjoy a visit to Holy Resurrection Cathedral in Tokyo (Nikolai-do) and Kandamyoujin Shrine close to Ginza, as well as Tokyo Station, whose brick walls have been recently restored. This area boasts a wonderful variety of famous destinations and popular spots.

たった九室だからできること

The potential of nine guest rooms

Ryumeikan is a hotel with only nine guest rooms. Japan's energized efforts to promote tourism have picked up over the last couple years, with the goal of annually attracting 20 million tourists by the time the Olympics and Paralympics are held in Tokyo in 2020. The year 2014 saw the number of tourists from abroad reach 13 million, and the number of repeat visitors to Japan is also on the rise. More and more people overseas are becoming interested in Japanese culture, and there is growing demand for experiences that fuse delicate Japanese sensibility with the strong spirit of the past, such as walks through historic towns, classical Japanese entertainment, *Budo* (the martial arts), and opportunities to dress up like shrine maidens. Ryumeikan is a Japanese-style town inn with great assets that have been passed down from previous landladies, such as comfortable sleep accommodations and spaces along with refined design. Ryumeikan offers the prestige of a brand and convenience of a hotel, while delivering value that makes it worth the trip to the Kanda-Ochanomizu area. We sincerely hope that our guests enjoy *geta* (clogs), *Shigarakiyaki* (ceramic) bathtubs, *furoshiki* (wrapping cloths) and *origami* (folding paper), all symbols of elegant and modern Japanese cultural sophistication. Ryumeikan is determined and makes it its mission to encourage as many foreign tourists as possible to discover and enjoy Japan through these experiences.

龍名館は十室に満たない客室数、たった九室のホテルです。二〇二〇年に東京開催が決定したオリンピック・パラリンピックに向け、年間二千万人の訪日外国人達成に向けて、日本国内の観光気運は高まっています。二〇一四年は、訪日外国人数が一三〇〇万人を突破。リピーターの数も増えつつあります。日本文化に関心を持っている外国人のお客さまも増えています。歴史的な街の散策や古典芸能や武道、中には巫女さん体験など、日本人の繊細で内に秘めた気骨な精神に触れることが求められています。龍名館は女将の真髄が連綿と受け継がれた街の旅館、快適な眠り、空間、そして洗練されたデザインを持ち合わせています。ホテルのブランドや利便性だけではなく、わざわざ神田・お茶の水に足を運んでいただく価値を提供することが、龍名館のできることなのです。お客様に下駄、信楽焼きのお風呂、風呂敷、折り紙など、奥ゆかしくもモダンな日本の文化をぜひ楽しんでいただきたい。そしてその体験から日本のファンになっていただくことが、龍名館の思いであり、やるべきことなのです。

お客さまと
ともに
和の心、
おもてなしの心で

Sharing wholehearted Japanese hospitality with guests

A hotel is a place for guests to relax and recover from the exhaustion of work or travel. Ryumeikan serves as a gateway for people to experience Japanese elegance and beauty while enjoying gorgeous accommodation, with our staff acting as travel guides for visitors. However, that does not mean we accompany them to their destination. We place a great deal of emphasis on supporting guests who take an active interest in Japanese culture through their experience at Ryumeikan. Our hotel is a true "town inn," so instead of providing routine services, we get closer to guests and support their trip by sharing in their experience. Ryumeikan stands as a space that is positioned between a hotel and home. We provide guests from abroad with the opportunity to enjoy Japanese housing spaces, lifestyle, and culture, things they cannot experience merely through sightseeing.

In August 2014, we made a new start under the name of Hotel Ryumeikan Ochanomizu Honten in the Kanda-Ochanomizu area. If you need our help, please feel free to ask our staff at any time. We are always committed to keeping a low profile and being reserved, running our establishment as a hotel that carries on the spirit of a traditional town inn.

ホテルは仕事や旅の疲れを癒し、休む場所です。そして龍名館は宿泊に加え日本の奥深い美しさに触れられる入口でもあります。スタッフはそのための旅先案内人です。明解な答えをお伝えするということではありません。龍名館をきっかけとして興味を持ったお客さまのサポートをすることを大切にしています。龍名館は「街の旅館」です。決まりきったマニュアル通りの接客をするよりも、親身に寄り添いお客さまと同じ感覚で旅のお手伝いをいたします。龍名館はホテルと自宅の間の存在です。観光だけでは分からない日本の住空間や日本人の暮らし、生活、文化を体験できます。分からないこと、困ったこと、いつでもスタッフにお声掛け下さい。でしゃばらず、控えめに―。そしてスタッフの根底にある"街の旅館の系譜を継ぐホテル"として。街の旅館は、平成二十六年八月、「神田・お茶の水」で「ホテル龍名館お茶の水本店」として、新たなスタートをきったのです。

龍名館で働く
スタッフが誇りを持てる
ホテルを創りたい

支配人 和賀茂樹

――和賀支配人は別名「ミスター龍名館」と言われるほど、まさに龍名館一筋ですね。

和賀 学生時代から旅行というよりホテルや宿泊施設に興味がありました。迷うことなく就職活動も宿泊業一本でしたね。国内のホテルや旅館、また都市型、リゾート型ホテルの就職説明会などでお話を聞く中で、龍名館と出会ったのです。

――なぜ、龍名館を選ばれたのですか。

和賀 小規模なホテルだからこそ、いろいろな体験ができると思いました。経営者に近い場所で働くことで、より広範の視点を持ちながらさまざまな業務に取り組み、所属部署の枠を超えた自己成長につながると考えました。料飲部や外部のパートナー企業など、一丸となってお客さまを迎えししなければなりません。また入社面接のときに、近い将来、東京駅八重洲に建つホテルの建て替え構想もあるという話を聞き、そのような場面に立ち会えることにとても魅力を感じました。

I want to make Ryumeikan a hotel that employees can be proud of.

General manager
Shigeki Waga

Q: I've heard that the honest and straightforward devotion to Ryumeikan you exhibit within your work has earned you the nickname "Mr. Ryumeikan."
Waga: I've been more interested in hotel and accommodation facilities than travel since my school days. I didn't hesitate to look for work in the accommodation business, and attended recruitment meetings held by domestic hotels, inns, and urban resort hotels. That's how I got to know Ryumeikan.

Q: Why did you choose Ryumeikan?
Waga: I felt that Ryumeikan's status as a small hotel would enable me to get a wide range of experience. My view was that working close to management would help me develop myself beyond the walls of hotel sections, and enable me to adopt a wider perspective when working on a range of operations. We have to work in close cooperation with restaurants and outside partners when we host guests. In addition, when I had my interview with Ryumeikan, I was lucky to hear about the upcoming plan for rebuilding a hotel near the Yaesu Gate of Tokyo Station in the near future. I was really interested in that opportunity.

Q: Ultimately you were involved in the full-scale rebuilding of the hotel near the Yaesu Gate of Tokyo Station and the recent renovation of the head building, being in charge of renewal project for the latter. How do you feel now after the renewed opening of the hotel?
Waga: Every day felt like a never ending series of trial and error as we worked to establish our concepts behind the hotel and present them to guests. Even after the hotel reopened, I spent many nights there myself checking to see if there were any problems in terms of the comfort of accommodations, or if there was anything that needed to be improved. Unlike the hotel with more than 100 guest rooms near the Yaesu Gate of Tokyo Station, the reopened hotel has only nine guest rooms, so each single room holds a great deal of significance for us. That being said, I feel that we are able to tap the potential of these nine rooms and determine how to share their appeal with guests.

Q: What's your future vision for the hotel?
Waga: My mission is to make improvements by lending an attentive ear to the feedback we receive from guests, and use it to create a hotel our employees can be proud of. In addition, we strive to make our hotel a major asset for the Kanda-Ochanomizu area, and place a great deal of emphasis on cooperating with the local community. We will continue to work hard with a sense of close-knit teamwork among the staff in our quest to become a hotel highly regarded both in Japan and around the world.

――東京駅八重洲口の全面建て替え、そして今回の本店の改装に立ち会い、本店においては責任者として指揮する立場で臨まれました。リニューアルオープンした今、心境はいかがですか。

和賀　ホテルコンセプトをどのように浸透させていくべきか、またお客さまにどのように響かせていくべきかなど試行錯誤の毎日です。リニューアルオープン後も私自身が何度も試泊を行い、快適に宿泊できる施設として不備がないか、また改善すべきことはないかなどチェックしていました。百室を超える東京・八重洲のホテルとは異なり、たった九室しかありませんので、一室の重みを強く感じます。しかし、逆に九室だからこそできることを見出し、きちんとお伝えしていくこともできます。

――将来的にどのようなホテルを目指しますか

お客さまの声を大切にし、改善するべきことは改善し、そして働く者たちが自慢でき、誇りに思えるホテルを創ることが私の使命でもあります。また地域との協調も図り、神田・お茶の水の資産となるホテル創りに努め、国内はもとより国際的な評価を獲得できるホテルを目指し、これからもスタッフ一丸となり取り組んでまいります。

百十余年の時を刻んでいる龍名館は神田駿河台の交差点近くにあります。そこはまさに文化の足跡が残る東京の中心地。龍名館の周辺は江戸時代より文化人が集う"日本のカルチェ・ラタン"なのです。神田川に架かる聖橋の美しいアーチを過ぎると、緑青をまとったドームの屋根が特徴的な「大聖堂・ニコライ堂」があります。昭和三十七年六月二十一日、国の重要文化財にも指定されています。駅の北側に進めば「史跡・湯島聖堂」や地域住民の憩い、集いの場である「神田明神」もあります。そしてノスタルジックな本と名喫茶の世界が広がる「神田・神保町」、専門書や古書のお店が立ち並んでいます。さらに東へ進むと世界中の観光客が訪れるにぎやかな「電気街・秋葉原」があります。最近はメイドのスタイルで出迎えてくれるメイドカフェや世界的に注目されているアニメや漫画など、ユニークなお店が発見できます。多種多様な文化が生まれ根づいてきた街、ぜひその足跡をたどってみてください。

Chapter 2: Welcome to Hotel Ryumeikan Ochanomizu Honten

Ryumeikan is located near the Kanda Surugadai crossing, and its history stretches back more than 110 years. The hotel's location is the exact center of Tokyo, and it retains many of the metropolis's cultural footprints. The area around our hotel is sometimes referred to as the "Quartier Latin of Japan" because cultured people have gathered there since the Edo period. Walking past the beautiful arch of the Hijiri Bridge over the Kanda River, you will soon catch sight of the Holy Resurrection Cathedral in Tokyo (Nikolai-do) with its distinctive greenish blue domed roof. This cathedral was designated as an important cultural property by the government on June 21, 1962. Traveling farther to the northern side of the station, you will come to Yushima Temple, a place rich in history, and Kanda Shrine, a place where local people like to gather and relax. Another must-visit spot is Kanda Jimbocho, a nostalgic area known for books and coffee houses. Its streets are lined with secondhand bookstores that sell specialty books and old antique books. In addition, if you walk further to the east, you will come to Akihabara, a famous destination for tourists from all over the world who come to shop in the home electric appliance stores along its bustling streets. In recent years Akihabara has become famous for its new type of unique shops, such as maid cafés where waitresses dressed in maid costumes serve customers, as well as shops featuring Japanese anime and manga that have attracted global interest. We highly recommend exploring the town's cultural landmarks and the great variety of entertainment establishments in the area around Ryumeikan.

龍名館の入り口にはご神木の「槐（えんじゅ）の木」があります。関東大震災（大正十二年）のとき、龍名館は火の粉の渦に巻き込まれ焼失してしまいました。この槐の木も焼けこげてしまいましたが、翌年、新芽を息吹いたのです。まさに大火で家を失った人々に "生きる" ことの強さを教え、勇気を与えてくれた木です。龍名館とともに百年を超えるときを過ごしてきた風格は、これからの龍名館の新たな時代を温かく見守ってくれているのです。

槐の木

中国原産。古くから台湾・日本・韓国などで植栽されています。和名は"えにす"から転化したものです。街路樹や庭木として植えられています。開花は七月で枝皮の円錐花序に白色の蝶形花を多数開きハチなどにとって、とても重要な蜜源植物です。また木質は固く、チョウナの柄として用いられています。

There is a sacred enju tree (pagoda tree) just in front of the Ryumeikan building. When the Great Kanto Earthquake struck Tokyo in 1923, our hotel was burned down in the fierce fires that swept across the city. This tree also suffered some fire damage, but the next year it sprouted new buds. In that sense, the tree symbolized the strength of "life" and gave courage to people who had lost their houses in the fires. The tree with its dignified presence has survived many difficulties together with Ryumeikan for more than 100 years, and will continue to offer us warm protection in the many years ahead.

Enju tree

The pagoda tree, which is native to China, has been cultivated since old times in Taiwan, Japan and South Korea. Its Japanese name is derived from the word "enisu." The tree is often seen planted along streets and in gardens. It blooms in July and produces many white butterfly-shaped flowers on its fluffy panicles. The flower is a significant source of honey for bees. The tree is extremely hard and tough, and for this reason its wood is used for the handles of cutting tools like a *chouna* (adze).

ホテル正面玄関を入ると古めかしくも威厳を感じさせる「旅館龍名館本店」の看板があります。この看板は関東大震災から建て直したときの看板です。お蔵から出てきました。その時の保存状態の良さから、"物を大切にする、もったいない"という先代たちの物をていねいにあつかう精神を感じました。看板の横にも旅館時代の欄間をアレンジし、お客さまをお迎えする顔として息を吹き返しました。宿帳を書いていただき、ご案内の準備ができるまで、温かいおしぼりとお茶で旅の疲れを癒してください。またフロントには自由に閲覧できるトラベルノートがあります。このノートは龍名館での滞在や旅の思い出を自由に綴っていただくものです。トラベルノートの記帳が増えることが私たちの願いです。創業百十余年の龍名館はこれまでも、これからもずっとこの地で営業を続けていきます。だから、もし今回の旅を思い出したとき、いつでもこのトラベルノートを見に来てください。龍名館はお客さまの第二の我が家、いつでも帰ってきてください。フロントの後ろにある本棚は"本の街"と言われた神田・神保町の街を象徴するものです。龍名館は地域とともに共生し、これからも、ともに生き続けていくという思いを込めています。

When you walk through the main entrance of our hotel, you will find an old-fashioned but dignified signboard that reads "Ryokan Ryumeikan Honten." This signboard was made when the hotel was rebuilt after the Great Kanto Earthquake of 1923. It was discovered in our warehouse in remarkably good condition. We were strongly impressed by the spirit of our predecessors for treating things with great care and affection. We also set up a curved wooden panel used for decoration in the early days of the ryokan just beside the signboard. This panel has found new life as the face that welcomes guests. After you check in, ease the exhaustion of your travel with a warm *oshibori* (hot towel) and flavored tea while you wait for us to finish the arrangements for your room. In addition, there is a travel notebook you can peruse at the front desk. You are more than welcome to write down memories of your travels and stay at Ryumeikan in this notebook. We sincerely hope more and more guests will add entries to this notebook. Ryumeikan, with a history stretching back 110 years, will continue to operate in this area just as it always has. Each time you think back on your trip, we hope you will come to take a look at the notebook again. Ryumeikan is your second home, so please feel free to come visit us any time. The bookshelf situated behind the front desk is representative of Kanda Jimbocho, which is well-known for being a "town of books." This bookshelf is a symbol of Ryumeikan's commitment to continue coexisting harmoniously with the local community.

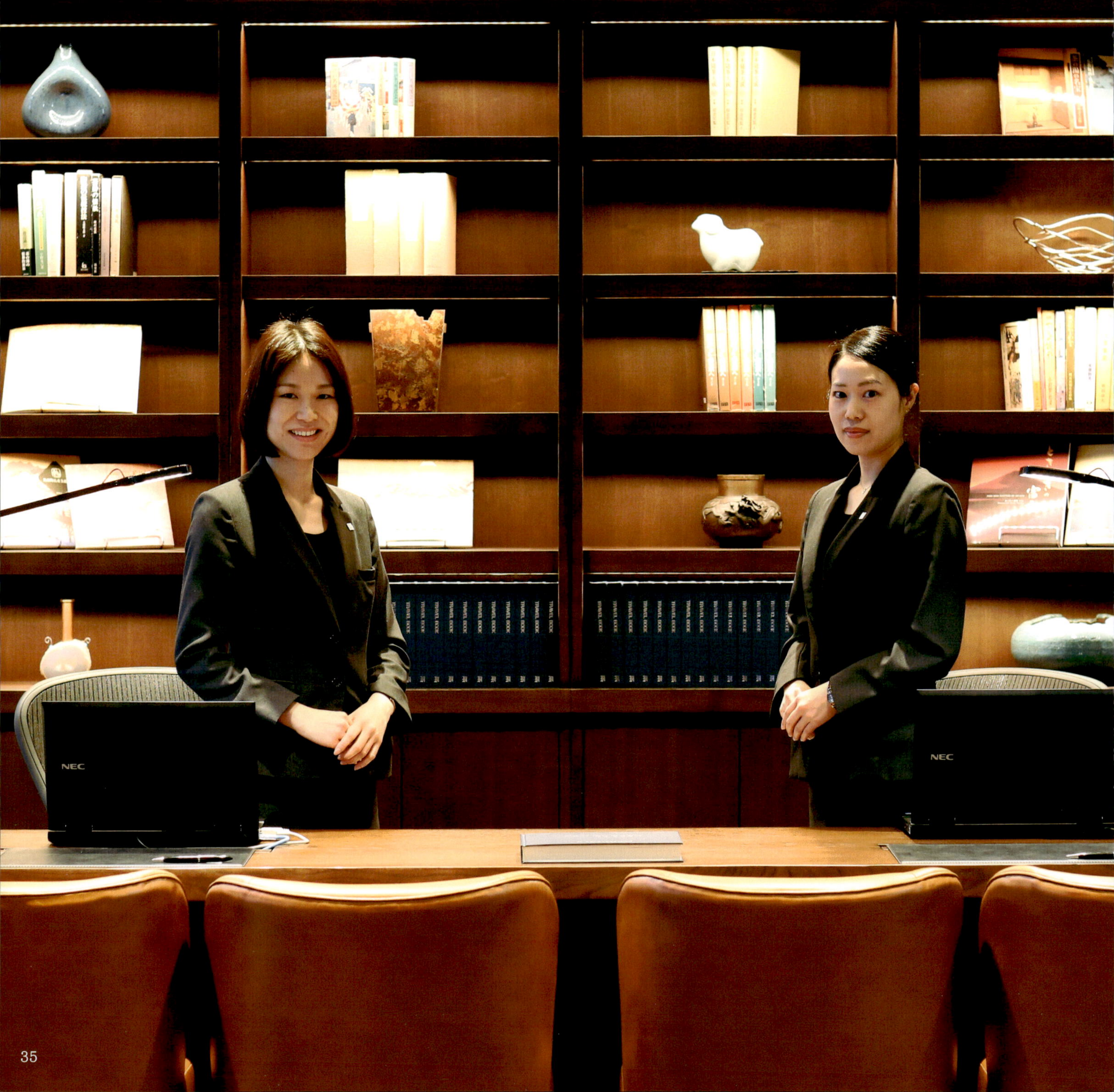

客室は二階にあります。九室のフロアガイドはアーティスト・ミヤケマイ氏により芸術作品の一つとして、デザインしていただきました。通路のカーペットは色とりどりの着物の帯が重なったイメージを表現。廊下の壁は日本家屋の建築をイメージして立体感のあるオフホワイト系で落ち着いた感じに仕上げました。

The guest rooms are on the second floor. The work of art on display, designed by the artist Mai Miyake, is a floor map depicting the nine rooms. The passageway carpet produces an image of colorful kimono obis (belts) lying on top of one another. We applied slightly yellowish white color coordinates to the wall of the corridor to create a three-dimensional yet harmonious atmosphere that evokes the essence of Japanese architecture.

37

北側と南側をつなぐ通路には大きな地図があります。この地図は江戸の古地図です。当時の街の様子や全体的な地形が分かります。一軒一軒の名前が綴られ、日本人の正確さ、きめ細かさを象徴する一枚です。現代の地図と比較しながら、当時の様子を思い描いてください。お部屋までわずかな距離ですが、それぞれ異なる世界に触れることができます。まさに日本文化の世界に入っていくエントランスなのです。フロアにはエレベーターを降りて左手にリフレッシュルーム、そしてこの通路の突き当りの左手にライブラリーをご用意しております。これらのスペースはチェックイン時間前にご到着されたお客さまや、ご滞在をより快適にされたいお客さまためのスペースです。長期滞在されるお客さまに、ランドリー設備もご用意しています。

There is a large map on the wall of the passageway linking the northern and southern sections of the hotel. This is an old map that depicts the towns and the landscape that existed in the Edo period (1603-1867). The names of each household are written on the map, which is a perfect indication of the Japanese's careful attention to precision and detail. Try to imagine the old Edo period by comparing this map with a contemporary one. Though it is only a short walk to your room, the passageway gives you the chance to enjoy these different images of the world. It is the perfect gateway to the world of Japanese culture. We also have a rest lounge to the left of the elevator and a library on the left at the end of the passage. These spaces are provided for guests who arrive before their check-in time and guests who want to enjoy a more comfortable stay. There are laundry facilities as well for extended-stay guests.

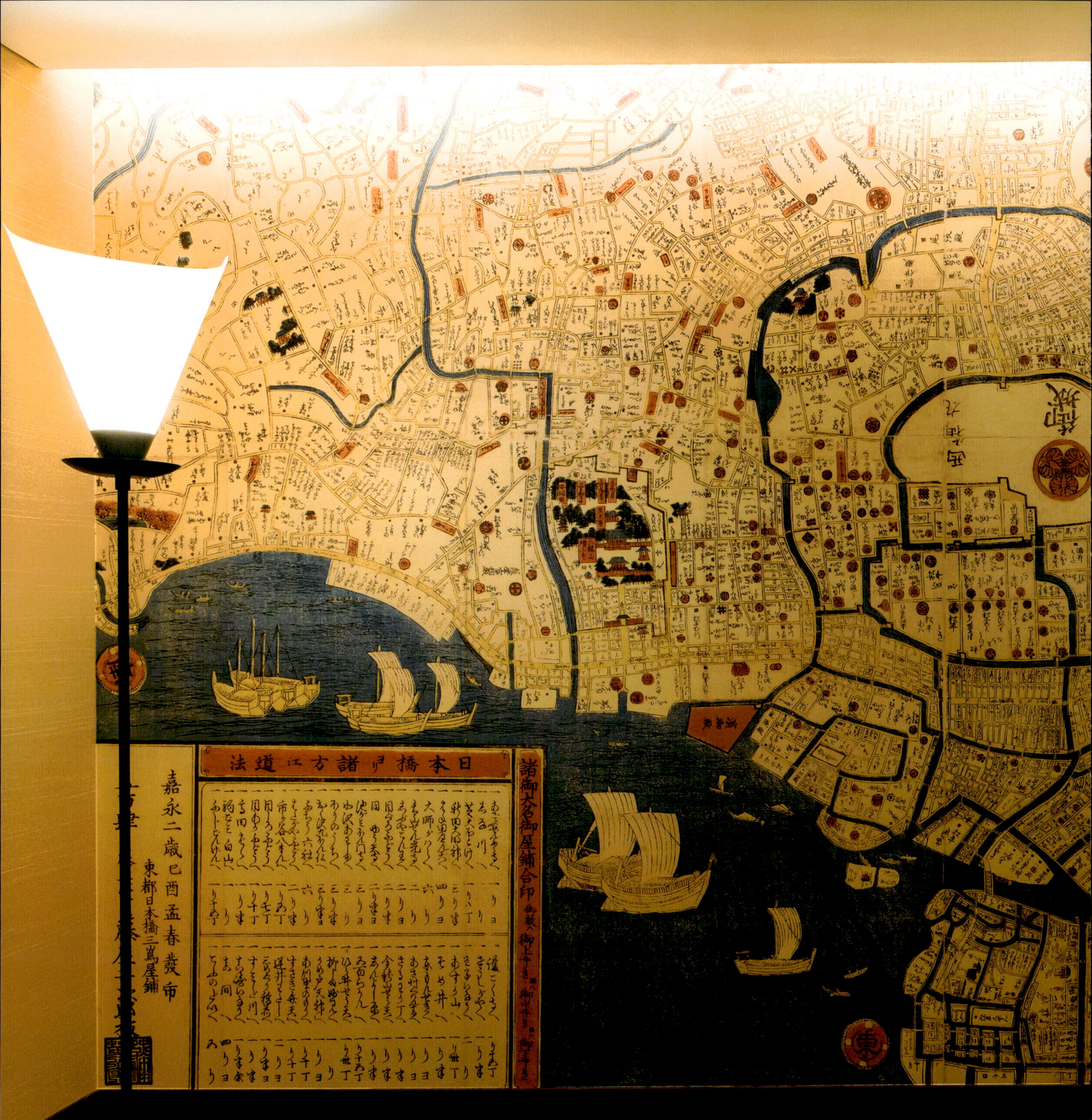
日本橋ゟ諸方江道法
諸御大名御屋鋪合印
嘉永二歳己酉孟春
東都日本橋三嶌屋鋪
東

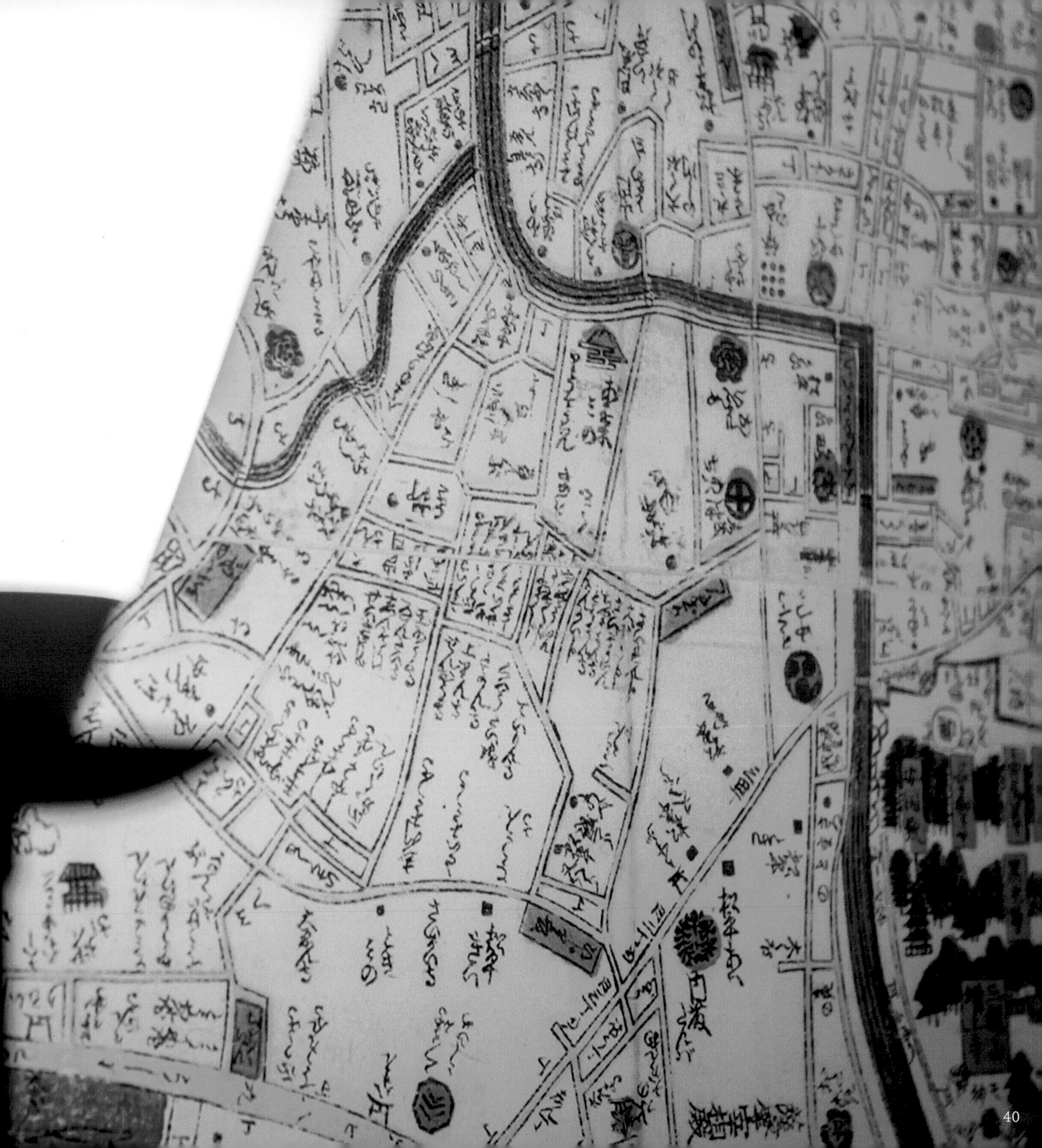

REFRESH ROOM

ライブラリーはご滞在中のお客さまに客室とは別の空間でリラックスできるスペースです。旅や日本文化などの情報を得られる場所としてさまざまな書籍をご用意しています。ライブラリーの窓からは近代的なビルやイチョウ並木、路を行き交う人や車など、神田・お茶の水の様子を間近に見ることができます。お飲み物やお菓子もご用意しています。ゆったりとした時間をお過ごしください。ライブラリーにある書籍はスタッフが選びました。客室のドアについている、部屋ごとに異なる鉄瓶を模したお部屋のサインは、ミヤケマイ氏にデザイン・制作いただいたものです。

The library is a space for guests to relax outside their rooms. It offers a variety of different books that can help you obtain information about travel and Japanese culture. From the library window, you can take in the sights of modern buildings, roadside maidenhair trees, and pedestrians and cars moving along the streets in the Kanda-Ochanomizu area. You can also help yourself to drinks and sweets. We hope you find the library to be the perfect place to relax. The books on display were selected by hotel staff members. The different signs featuring an iron kettle set on the doors of the guest rooms were designed and created by the artist Mai Miyake.

43

客室サインは、お茶の水の地名から「急須」のデザインに

アーティスト　ミヤケマイ氏

——龍名館さんのお話をプロデューサーの芹沢様からお声をかけていただきました。歴史をお聞きすると、もともとは旅籠から始められたとのことなので、お茶の水という地名からインスピレーションを得て、客室名と客室名サインを制作しました。当初、龍名館さんは一般的な客室番号での表示をお考えでしたが、お部屋の名前は旅館のヘリテージを表すために、前にお使いになられていたものから使うのがいいかと考え、ご提案しました。本店からは「銀杏」「松」「桐」。八重洲からは「桜」「藤」「蘭」「菊」「百合」「牡丹」。すべて植物でかつ日本的な物を選びました。それは外国人にも説明がしやすいものがいいかなと思っての選考です。また外国の方に名前を覚えていただくためにも、お部屋の名前である花や植物の名前を漢字と、英語名での表記ではなく、読みをそのままローマ字表記にいたしました。客室サインのアートワークにつきましては、龍名館にちなんで「龍」、お茶を食すというレストランコンセプトと地名から「急須」、そして客室名ごとの

Photo:Shoji Onuma

Guest room signs bearing an image of a "*kyusu* (small teapot)" in reference to the name Ochanomizu (*ocha* for "tea")

Designer Mai Miyake

Mr. Serizawa, the producer of the Ryumeikan renewal project, contacted me with an offer to do some design work. I was familiar with the hotel's history of originally being a "*hatagoya*" (a type of Japanese inn where travelers stayed in old times). I drew inspiration from the name Ochanomizu and created the guest room names and signs. Initially, Ryumeikan thought of merely assigning a number to each guest room, but I told them that the naming of the rooms was a way to reflect the hotel's ryokan heritage, and proposed using some of the names they had used in the past. From the head inn, I selected "*Icho* (ginko)," "*Matsu* (pine)," and "*Kiri* (paulownia)," and from Yaesu inn, I chose "*Sakura* (cherry tree)," "*Fuji* (wisteria)," "*Ran* (orchid)," "*Kiku* (chrysanthemum)," "*Yuri* (lily)," and "*Botan* (peony)." These are all plants that represent Japanese characteristics, and the reason that I chose these names was because they better convey these characteristics to people from other countries. In addition, I used Chinese characters and Roman letters, not English words, to express the flower and plant names of the rooms so that guests from abroad could remember them more easily. For the room sign artwork, I noted the combination of "*ryu* (dragon)" for Ryumeikan, "*kyusu* (small teapot)" for the concept of a tea restaurant and the name "Ochanomizu," the place where the hotel is located, and the icons for each guest room name. I also applied the rusty color of an iron kettle to the entire sign to create a distinctive Japanese atmosphere that guests could enjoy. The water *ryu* (dragon) is believed to help deter fire, so I decided to include an image of the water dragon featured on Ryumeikan tags in the past within my art work as a type of prayer for keeping this accommodation facility safe from disaster. * Toshio Hamada stated that his father told him that the dragon could protect buildings from fire. I was greatly impressed with Ryumeikan staff's passionate care and affection for nice old things. In recent years these kinds of things have been destroyed and replaced with a steady stream of new buildings. If this trend continues, we will see amazing Japanese culture lose its appeal and vanish. I think that it is both extremely rare and important that Ryumeikan is devoted to passing on the nice things, culture, and essence of Japan to younger generations for more than 100 years.

「アイコン」で構成しました。またサイン全体は鉄瓶の錆びた色合いにし、日本独特の雰囲気を醸し出すことで日本の雰囲気に触れていただければいいなと思います。いることから、宿泊施設として防災の願掛けで龍名館で過去に使われていた荷札に描かれていた水龍をアートワークに組み込みました（浜田敏男談 過去に父より"龍は火事から建物を守る"と言われたことがある）。龍名館のスタッフのとても熱心に古き良きものを大切にされている姿勢に感銘を受けました。最近は古き良きものが壊され、次から次へと新たしい建物が造り上げられています。このままでは本当に素晴らしい日本文化の影が薄くなってしまいます。龍名館さんのように百年のときを越えても日本の良きもの、文化、心を伝えていくという考えはとても希有なことだと思います─

アーティスト　ミヤケマイ氏
日本の伝統的な美術や工芸の繊細さや奥深さに独自のエスプリを加え、過去と現在、未来までをシームレスにつなげながら物事の本質を問う作品を制作。媒体を問わず骨董、工芸、現代アート、「デザインなど既存のジャンルを問わずに天衣無縫に制作発表。大分県立美術館

Photo:Satoshi Shigeta

has also worked on commissioned works, such as for Ginza Maison Hermès, TOTO at Tokyo Designers Week, and Banraisha Gallery of Keio University's Hiyoshi Campus. She received a scholarship at Ecole Nationale Superieure des Beaux-Arts (Paris, France) from 2008-2009. Three books of her collections have been published, including *Maku Meiro: Down the Rabbit Hole* (Hatori Press, Inc. 2012).
www.maimiyake.com

Photo:Satoshi Shigeta

アーティストと
龍名館の
思いをつなぎ、
まとめていく

プロデューサー　芹沢高志氏

——ホテル龍名館お茶の水本店のリニューアルにおいてプロデューサーとしてかかわってきました。私はデザイナーでもなく、ホテル関係者でもなく、役目は龍名館の方々の思いと、アートディレクターの大良さんの思い、考えを創造的に調整することです。私自身は、元々都市・地域計画に従事してきたものです。それがひょんなことから現代アートに深く関わることになり、今ではさまざまな地域の芸術祭のディレクターを務めたりもしています。その中で今回、客室名や客室サインに関してミヤケマイさんをご紹介するなど、現代アートとの融合も試みました。ホテル龍名館お茶の水本店が建つ地域は、江戸情緒あふれる庶民文化、龍名館、そして大学も多々ある中での学生文化、そして百十余年培ってきた龍名館そのものの文化、龍名館を取り巻く地域の文化、そして共生など、さまざまな日本文化が今もなお継承されている地域です。この素晴らしい文化を"学び"を開発コンセプトに発信していきたいという龍名館さんの思いと、アーティストとして表現したい雰囲

ideas of art director Taira. Personally, I originally did work in urban and community planning, but later had the opportunity to become deeply involved in contemporary art. Today, I direct regional art festivals. For the recent project, I introduced Ms. Mai Miyake as the designer for guest room names and signs, and sought to fuse the design aspects of the project with contemporary art. The area where Hotel Ryumeikan Ochanomizu Honten is located possesses a rich and varied Japanese cultural heritage. There is popular culture that conjures images of the old Edo atmosphere, student culture with the many universities nearby, the culture of Ryumeikan itself and its more than 110 years of history, the community culture surrounding Ryumeikan, and its coexistence with local communities. As a producer, it was my job to play a central role in coordinating the different factors based on the development concept of "learning," such as Ryumeikan's passion for disseminating these wonderful forms of culture, with the atmosphere, colors, texture, ideas, and preferences the designer wanted to express, and facilitate the entire collaborative process by getting everyone on the same page.

気、色合い、質感、考え方、好き嫌いなど、さまざまな要素をすり合わせ、相互納得の上で全体をまとめていくのがプロデューサーとして求められたことです。

撮影：久保貴史／©別府現代芸術フェスティバル2009実行委員会

しかも九室、二フロアという限られた空間の中でどのように表現していくのか、逆に九室だからできることは何なのかなど、非常に研ぎ澄まされた一本筋のあるアートが求められます。感覚的な統一感がなければ九室しかないだけに崩れてしまいます。つまり龍名館さん側が描いている"学ぶ"という開発コンセプト、神田・お茶の水という新名所を作り上げていくという思いを岩盤に構築することが実現できません。消耗品やステーショナリーにもこだわり、美的統一感を作り上げるまでが今回のプロジェクトのひと山だったと思います。今回の仕事を通じて龍名館さん、そしてアートディレクターを担当した大良さんを通じ、改めて日本文化とエリアとの共生、地方創生のつなぐ、人を育てていくホテルの役割を実感しましたね。今後ますます地域との共生、人を声が高まる中で、地域に根ざしたホテル、そして地域に伝わるさまざまなアート、文化が持つ力が求められることでしょう。

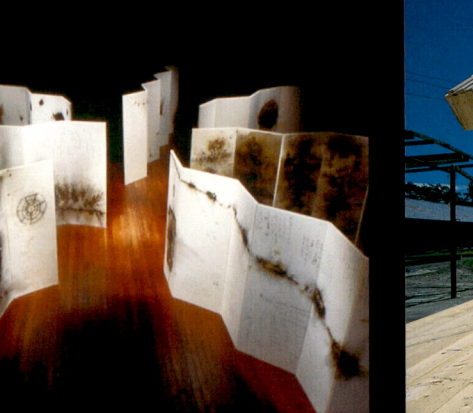

撮影：萩原美寛

撮影：萩原美寛

撮影：細川浩伸

撮影：萩原美寛

I was required to produce keenly refined art, with the main challenge being how to maximize the potential of nine rooms and express the project concept within the limited space of these nine rooms and two floors. If I failed to create a consistent and unified sense, I would end up ruining the entire expressive theme with the nine rooms available. Essentially, that meant I wouldn't be able to realize the ideal form based on Ryumeikan's development concept of "learning" and passion for transforming the Kanda-Ochanomizu area into a new tourist destination. One of our major challenges was in creating aesthetic unity and consistency with a keen focus on consumables and stationery. Through the last joint project with Ryumeikan and art director Taira, I truly recognized the importance of the hotel's role in facilitating the coexistence of Japanese culture and local communities, and for connecting people and helping them grow. As the call for regional coexistence and revitalization grows stronger, more and more people will need locally planted hotels and the power of different regional arts and culture.

Producer Takashi Serizawa

Takashi Serizawa was born in Tokyo in 1951. After graduating from the Department of Mathematics of the Graduate School of Science at Kobe University and the Department of Architecture and Building Science of the College of Engineering at Yokohama National University, Serizawa engaged in research on ecological land utilization planning as part of a regional planning team. Following this, he was involved in the construction project of a large *sangharama* at Tochoji Temple in Yotsuya, Tokyo, and established P3 art and environment in 1989. He carried out various art and environmental projects from the underground hall in the precincts of Tochoji Temple until 1999, and since 1999 he has worked on projects at number of other places. He established a project space in a building in front of Tochoji Temple in 2014. He has held numerous posts over the course of his career, including executive director of the Tokachi International Contemporary Art Exhibition "Demeter" held at Obihiro Horse Racing Track (2002), director of the Asahi Art Festival (from 2003 to the present), the curator of Yokohama Triennale 2005, executive director of the Beppu Contemporary Art Festival "Mixed Bathing World" (2009, 2012, and 2015), and the Executive Director of the Design and Creative Center Kobe (KIITO) (from 2012 to the present). He was also appointed the director of Saitama Triennale 2016 in July 2014. He is the author of *Moving in Our Planet* (Iwanami Shoten Publishers), A View from the Moon (Mainichi Shimbun), and *Beppu* (the Steering Committee of the Beppu Contemporary Art Festival 2015 'Mixed Bathing World'). He also translated into Japanese *Operating Manual for Spaceship Earth* by R. Buckminster Fuller (Chikumashobo Ltd.), *The Self-Organizing Universe: Scientific and Human Implications of the Emerging Paradigm of Evolution* by Erich Jantsch (Kousakusha), and *The Starship and the Canoe* by Kenneth Brower (Yama-kei Publishers Co., Ltd.).

プロデューサー　芹沢高志氏

1951年東京生まれ。神戸大学理学部数学科、横浜国立大学工学部建築学科を卒業後、（株）リジオナル・プランニング・チームで生態学的土地利用計画の研究に従事。その後、東京・四谷の禅寺、東長寺の新伽藍建設計画に参加したことから、89年にP3 art and environmentを開設。99年までは東長寺境内地下の講堂をベースに、その後は場所を特定せずに、さまざまなアート、環境関係のプロジェクトを展開している。2014年より東長寺対面のビルにプロジェクトスペースを新設。帯広競馬場で開かれたとかち国際現代アート展「デメーテル」総合ディレクター（02年）、アサヒ・アート・フェスティバル事務局長（03年～）、横浜トリエンナーレ2005キュレーター、別府現代芸術フェスティバル「混浴温泉世界」総合ディレクター（09年、12年、15年）、デザイン・クリエイティブセンター神戸（KIITO）センター長（12年～）などを務める。2014年7月、さいたまトリエンナーレ2016のディレクターに就任。著書に『この惑星を遊動する』（岩波書店）『月面からの眺め』（毎日新聞社）、『別府』（別府現代芸術フェスティバル「混浴温泉世界」実行委員会）、訳書にバックミンスター・フラー『宇宙船地球号操縦マニュアル』（ちくま学芸文庫）、エリッヒ・ヤンツ『自己組織化する宇宙』（共訳：工作舎）、ケネス・ブラウワー『宇宙船とカヌー』（ヤマケイ文庫）など。

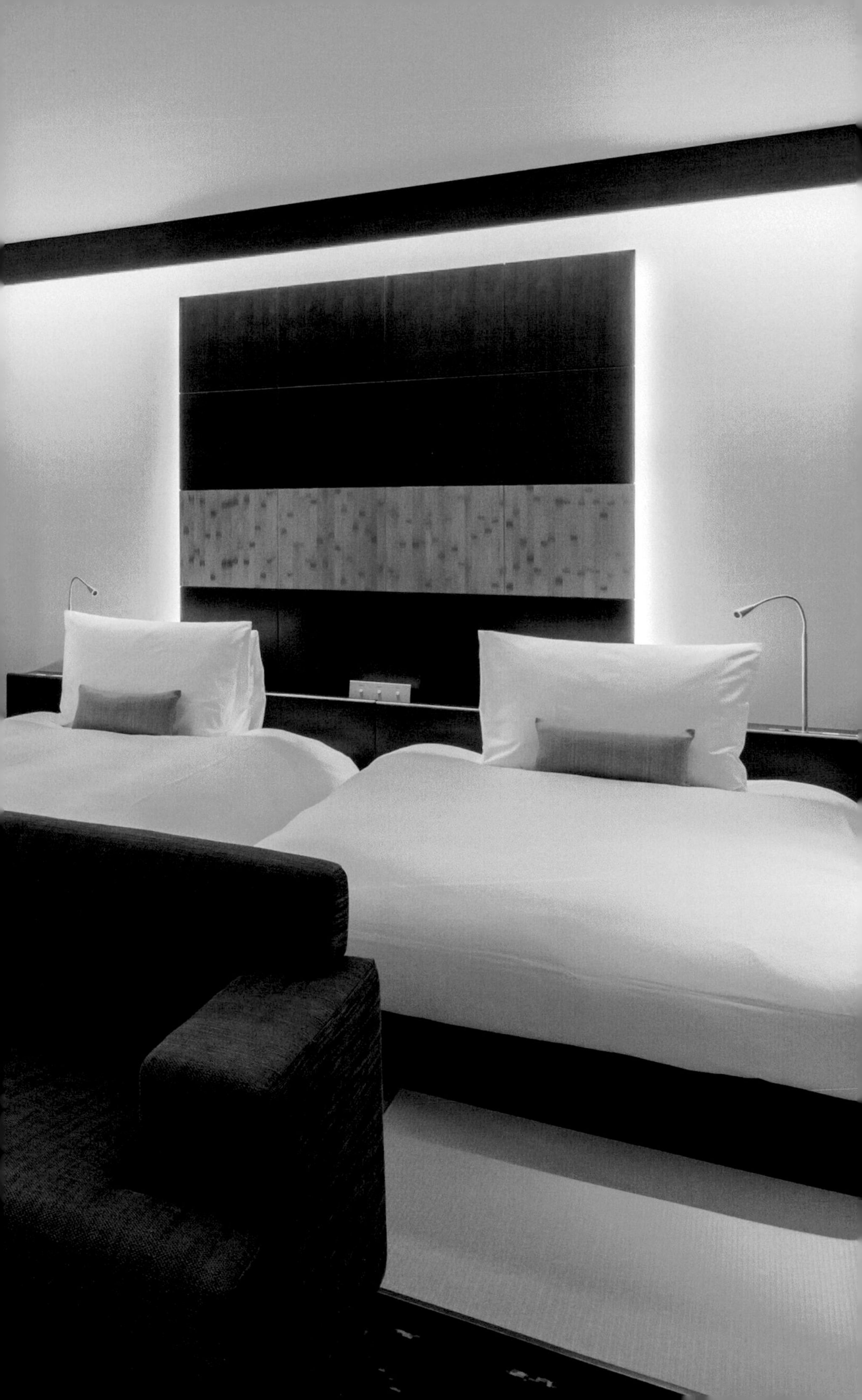

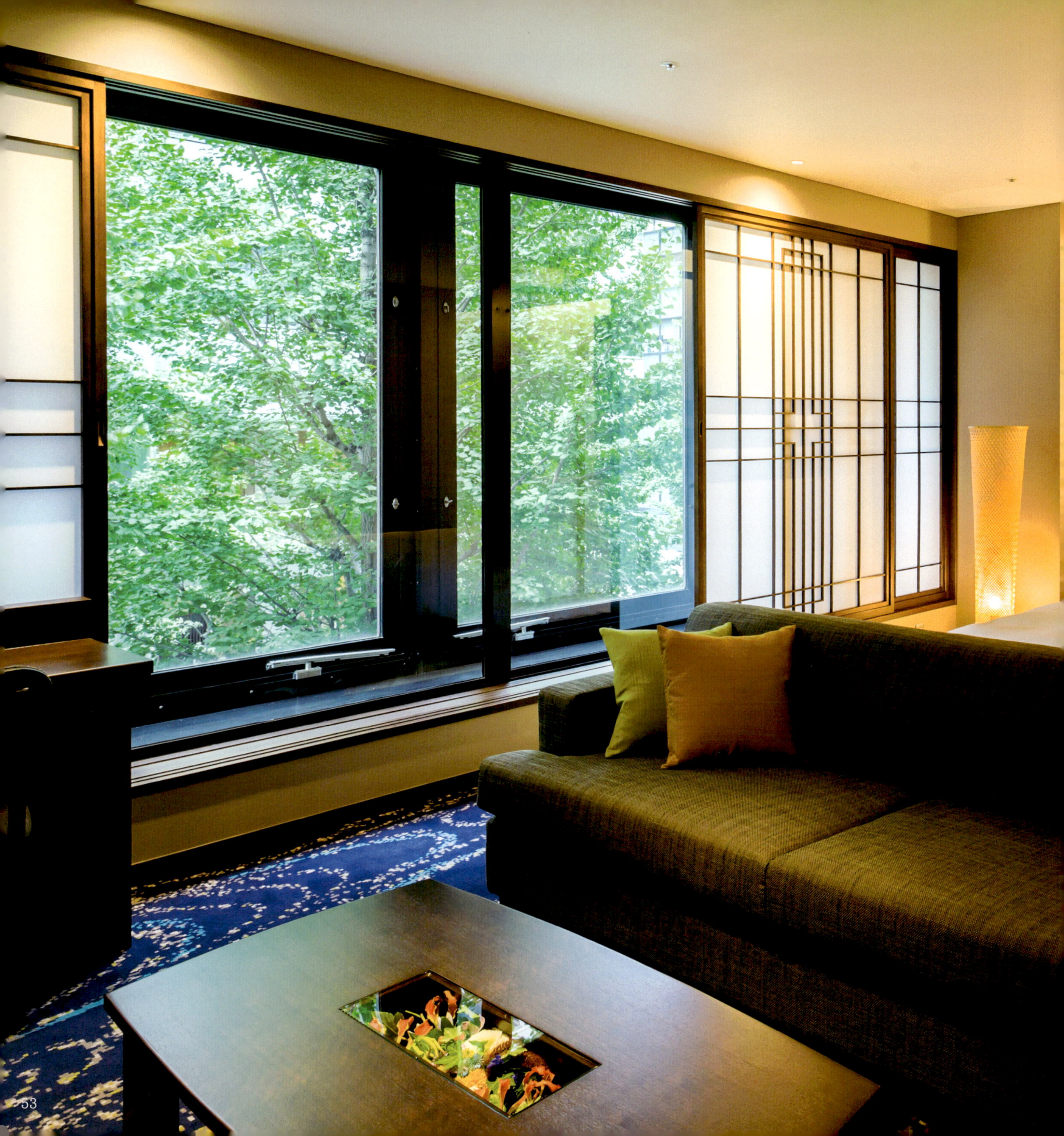

客室に入るとまず目に入るのは玄関と昔ながらの引き戸です。物静かな感じですが、お客さまを迎え入れる日本ならではのスタイルを再現いたしました。玄関横の下駄箱には、ぜひ神田・お茶の水の街を下駄を履いて歩く時間を楽しんでいただきたいとの思いから、日本で伝統的な履物である下駄をご用意させていただきました。お部屋へ上がる際には靴を脱いでお上がりください。靴を脱ぐというのも日本ならではの習慣です。畳のお部屋も日本家屋ならではのものです。

Chapter 3: A Guide to the Guest Rooms of Hotel Ryumeikan Ochanomizu Honten

When you enter a guest room, the first thing you see is the front door and traditional Japanese sliding doors. These create a quiet atmosphere and express our wish to convey an original Japanese style that welcomes guests. We provide *geta* (Japanese wooden clogs) in the *geta* box at the front door so that guests can enjoy walking around the Kanda-Ochanomizu area wearing traditional Japanese footwear. We also ask for our guests to take off their shoes when they enter their room. Taking off one's shoes is a common Japanese custom. Rooms with tatami mat flooring are also typical of a traditional Japanese residence.

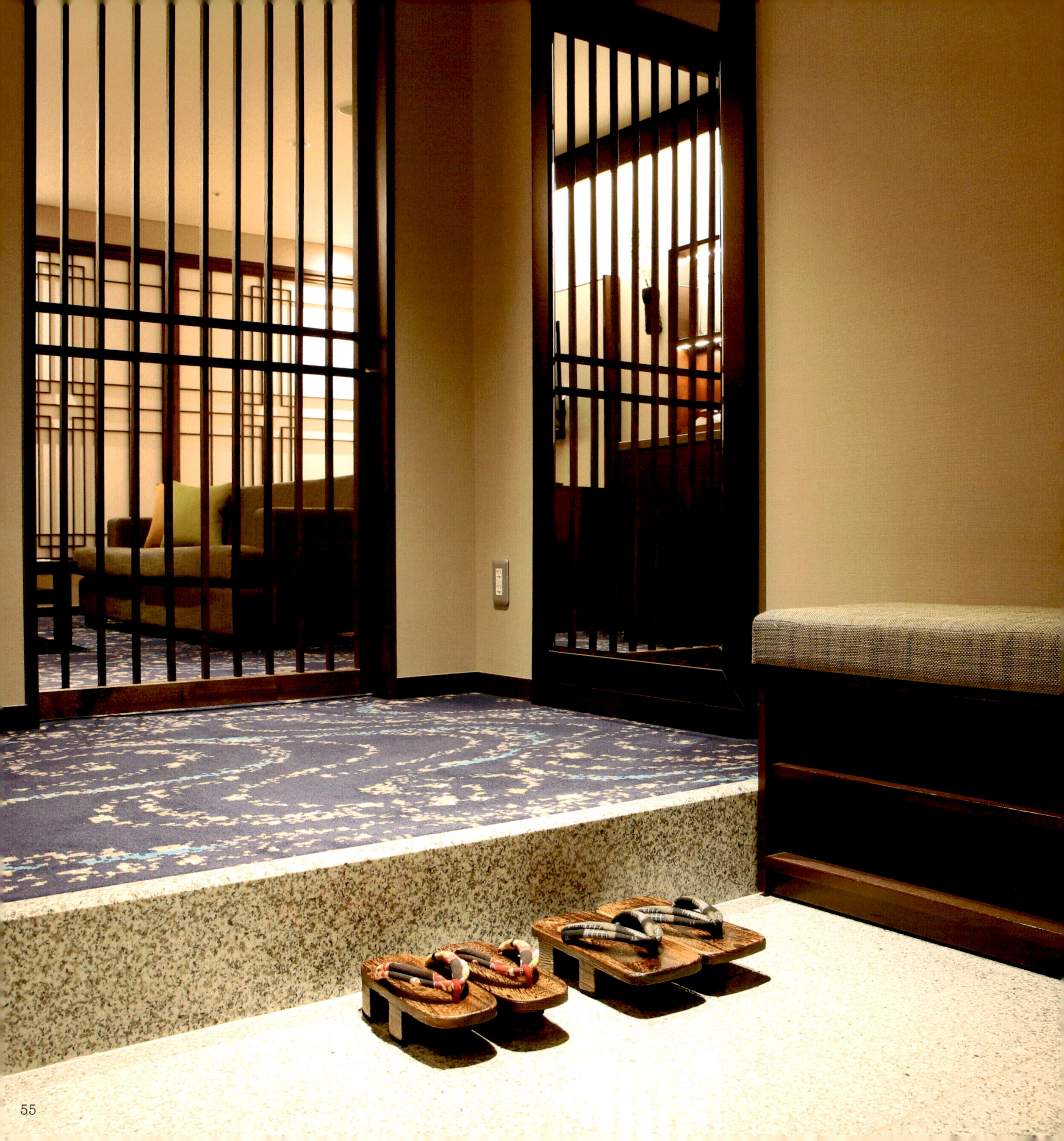

入って正面にある障子の繊細な障子柄は、過去の旅館時代のデザインを復刻したものです。客室のルームキーのデザインや、風呂敷のデザインにも取り入れています。カーペットは畳の黄金色の補色である群青色（ぐんじょういろ）でアレンジしています。デザインはお茶の水の名にちなみ水紋柄を取り入れました。お部屋の家具は胡桃色（くるみいろ）を使うなど日本独特な色を使ってデザインされています。

The delicate patterns of the *shoji* (traditional Japanese sliding paper doors) right at the front of the room are a replication of the past designs we used when the hotel was a ryokan. We adopted the same style for the designs of guest room keys and *furoshiki* (a wrapping cloth) as well. Lapis lazuli coordinates have been applied to the carpet as a color to complement the golden hues of the tatami. For the carpet design, we selected water ring patterns in reference to the name of Ochanomizu (*mizu* is Japanese for "water"). For furniture design, we used walnut coloring to create an atmosphere of colors unique to Japan.

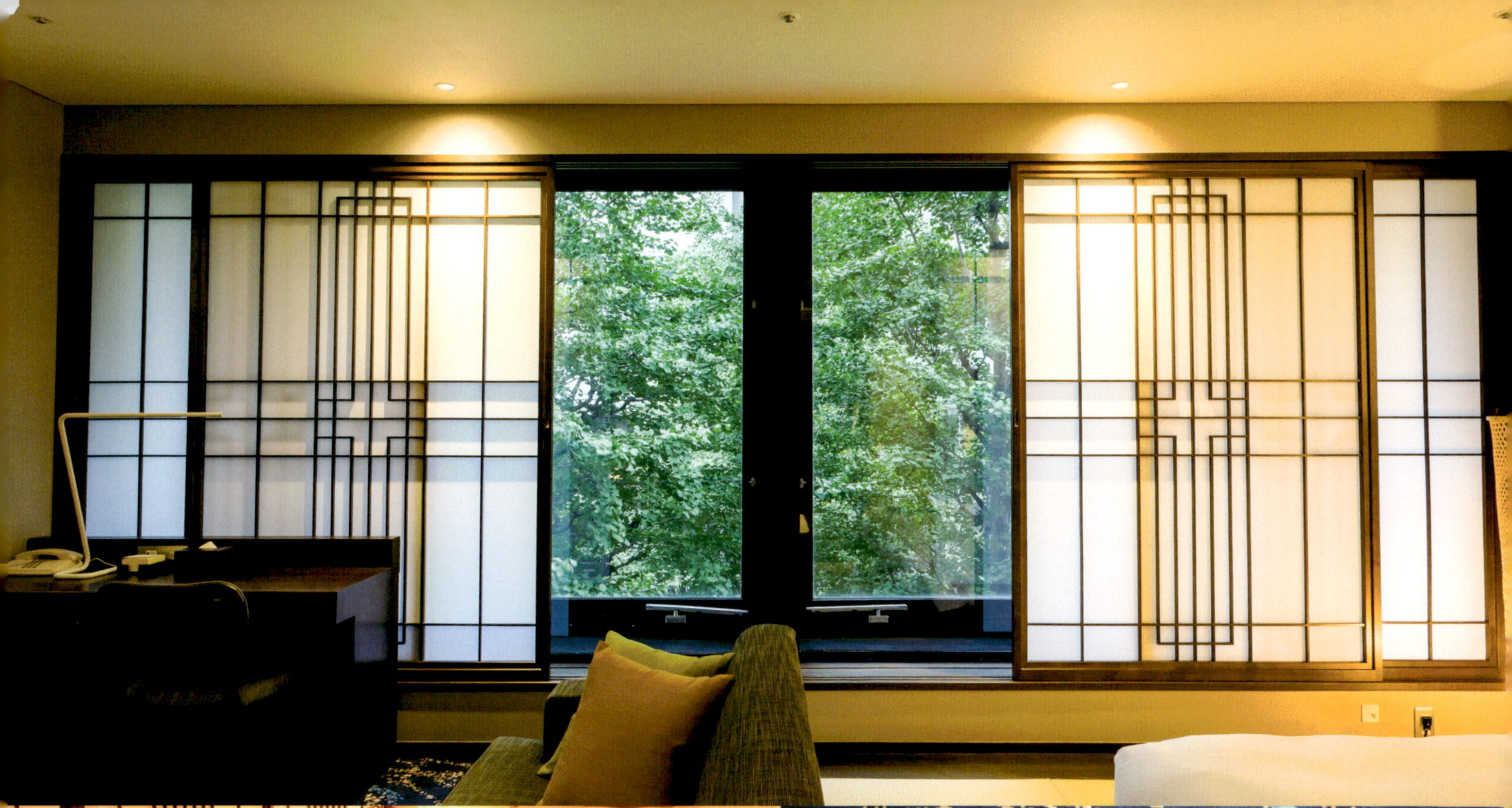

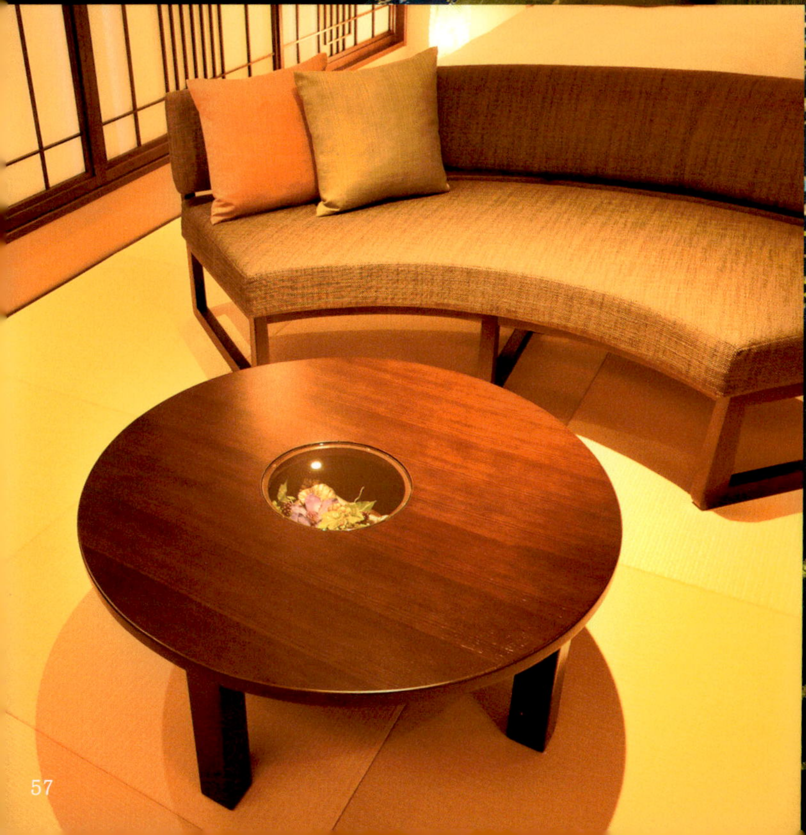

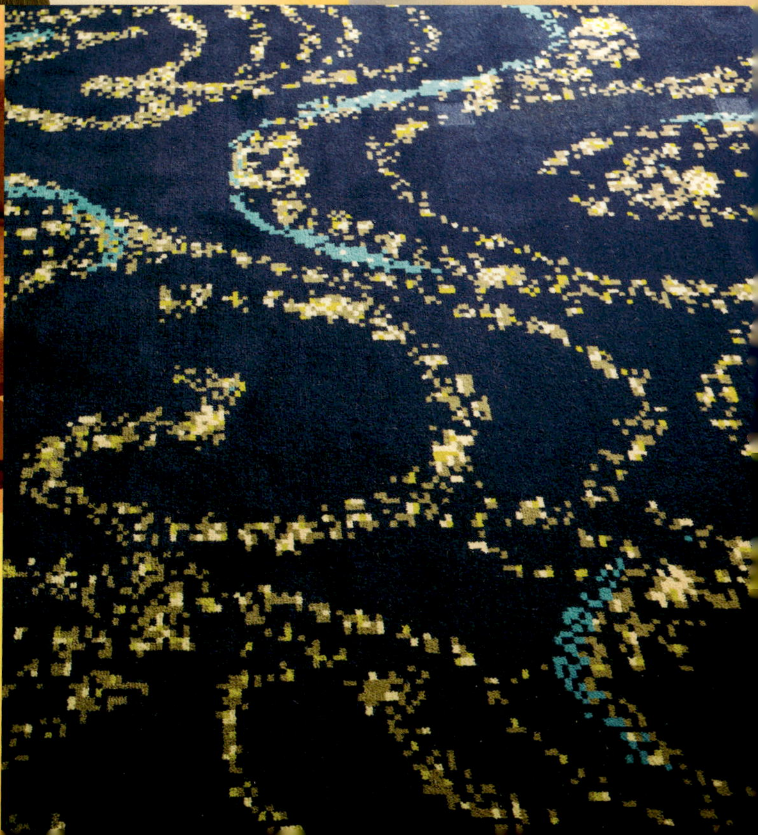

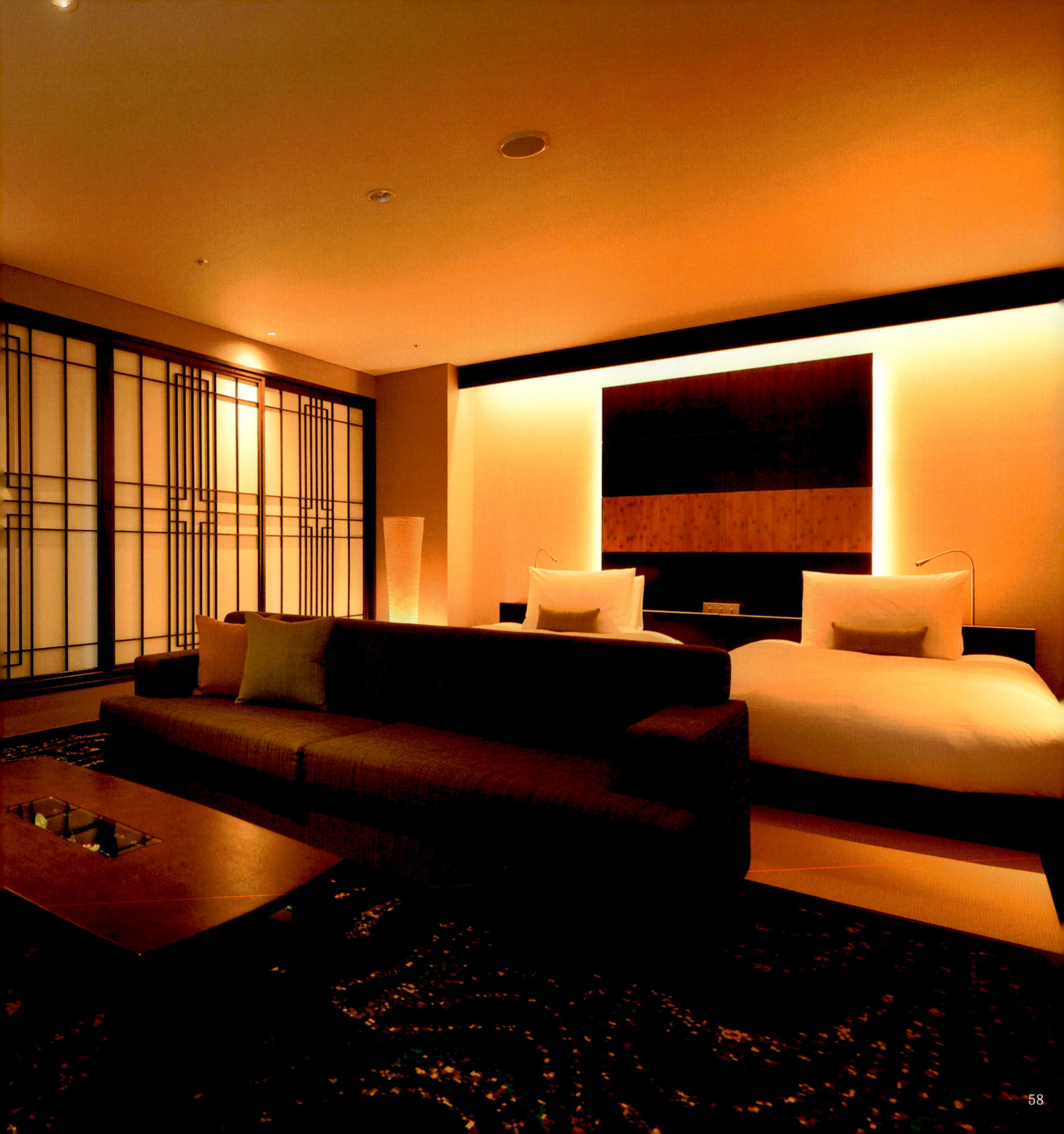

インテリアコンセプトとしてさまざまなキーワードが挙げられました。

陰翳礼讃（いんえいらいさん）

わびさび

先鋭的な都会と共存している「東京の和」

四季

物をていねいにあつかう精神

収納の文化

陰翳礼讃は谷崎潤一郎の随筆「経済往来」（昭和八年）に掲載されたものです。まだ電灯のなかった時代の今日とちがった美の感覚を論じたものです。西洋では可能な限り部屋を明るくして陰翳を消すことに執着しましたが、日本ではむしろ陰翳を認め、それを利用することで陰翳の中でこそ映える芸術を作り上げてきました。それこそが日本の芸術の特徴であることを主張したものです。この主張のもと、建築、照明、紙、食器、食べ物、化粧、能や歌舞伎の衣裳など、多岐にわたって陰翳の考察がなされています。この思想から間接照明を各所に取り入れ、ホテルと住宅の中間的なリラックスできる空間を作りあげました。

We came up with a number of key phrases to describe our interior concept.
In praise of shadows
Wabi-sabi (appreciation and admiration of the belief that objects gain value through use and age)
Tokyo *wa* (Japanese style): Coexistence with the vibrant urban environment
Four seasons
The spirit of treating things with great care and affection
The culture of storage

Novelist Junichiro Tanizaki wrote "In Praise of Shadows" in his essay *Keizai Ohrai* in 1933. In this piece, he discussed a sense of beauty in an era without electrical lighting systems that is different from that of today. He commented that people in the west strove to make rooms as bright as possible and drive out all shadows. In contrast, Japanese people recognized the value of shadows, taking full advantage of their qualities to create art that looks even better shrouded in shadows. Tanizaki claimed that this use of shadows was a distinct characteristic of Japanese art. Based on this recognition, he presented a wide variety of observations about shadows, focusing on their presence in architecture, lighting, paper, dishes, food, cosmetics, and Noh and Kabuki costumes. Working in line with this view, we introduced forms of indirect lighting at many spots to produce a relaxing environment that stands between a hotel and home.

60

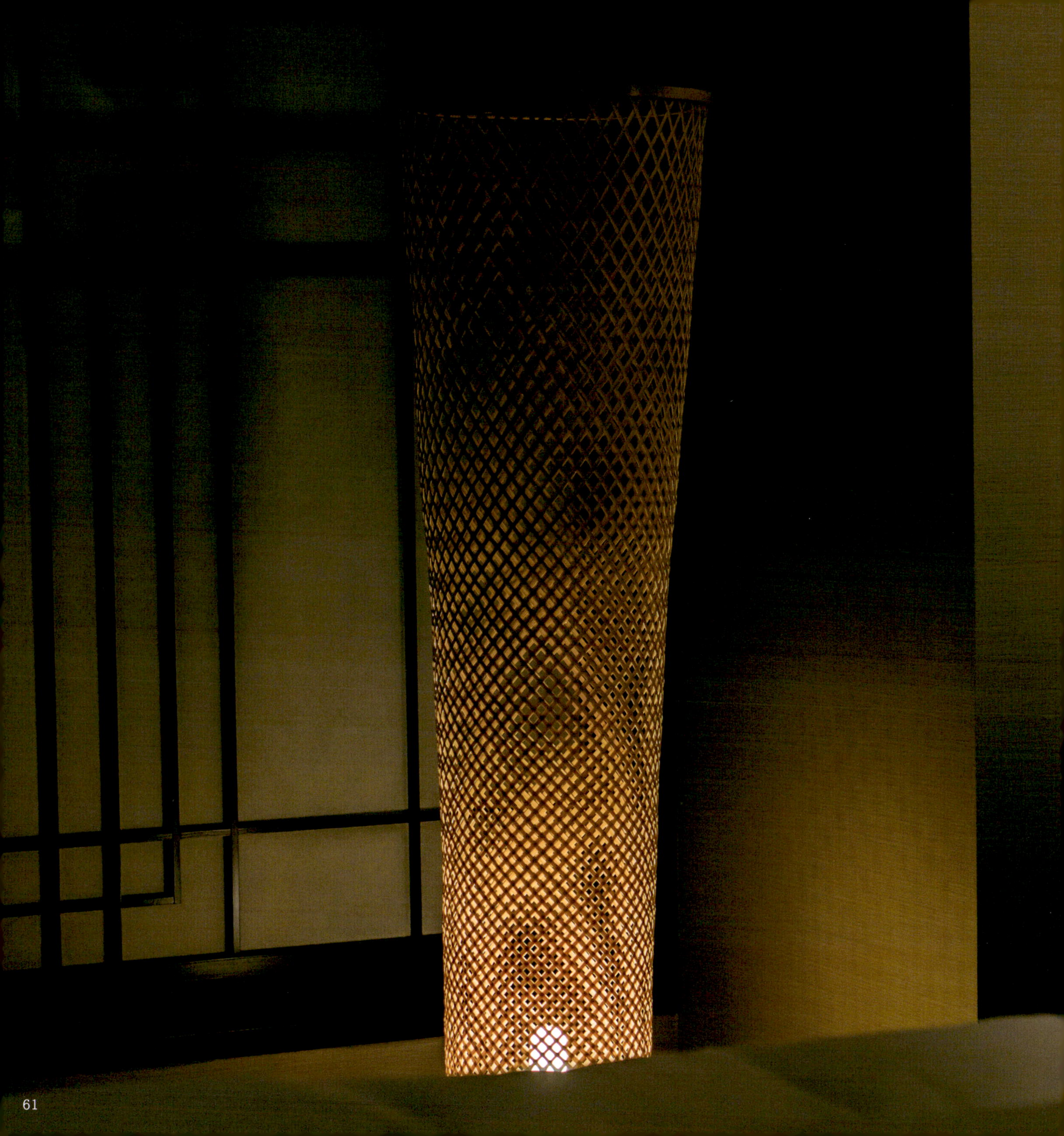

お風呂はすべてのお部屋に滋賀県の信楽焼きの陶器風呂をご用意。日本のお風呂に欠かせない風呂桶もご用意しています。さらに和をテーマとした入浴剤もお試しください。体の芯から温まります。また機能性も追求し、マッサージ機能付きシャワーもご用意しておりますので、ご滞在中、日本のお風呂文化を感じていただけます。バスタオルは温まった体を包みこむような優しさとぬくもりを与えてくれる愛媛県の「今治タオル」をタオルソムリエに選定していただきました。

Shigarakiyaki ceramic bathtubs (from Shiga Prefecture) are installed in all of our guest rooms. We also have bath basins, an essential item for Japanese bathing. Please try bath salts designed to place an emphasis on *wa* (Japanese style) as well. They will help warm your body to the core. In addition, we also have massaging showers that help deliver the functionality you need to enjoy Japanese-style bathing during your stay. For our bath towels, we provide Ehime prefecture-made "Imabari towels," which are specially selected by a towel sommelier. These towels create a sense of softness and warmth when they are wrapped around the body.

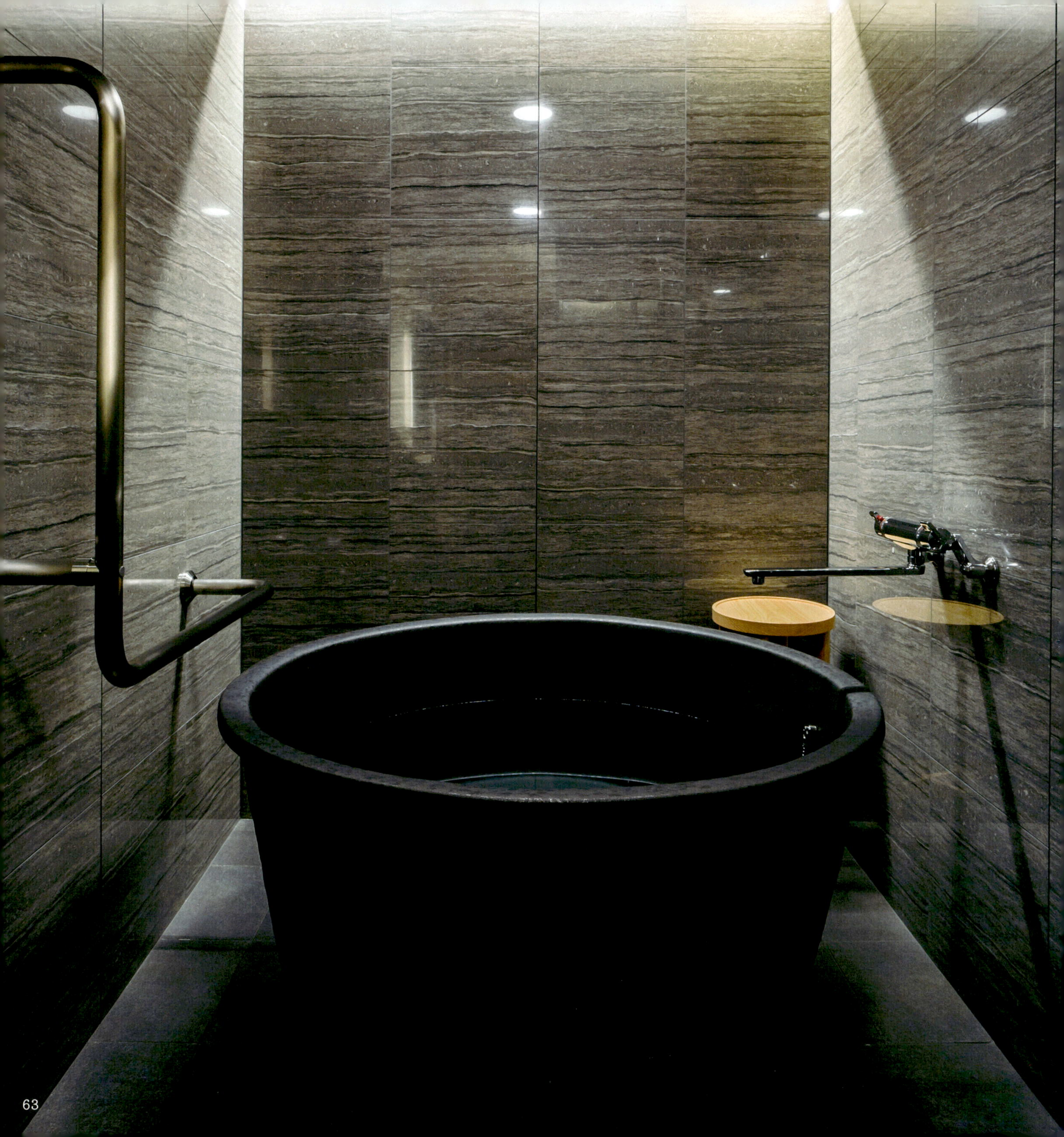

陶器独特のわびさび、ぬくもりを

信楽焼き陶器浴槽 丸元製陶
代表取締役 村木郁夫氏

—信楽焼きと言うと、どうしてもタヌキの置き物というイメージが強く、実際、この地域ではタヌキの信楽焼きをあちこちで販売されていますね。

村木 はい、当社はこの信楽という土地に陶器製造メーカーとして生まれ四十年余、これまでの経験、培った技術を生かし、「信楽焼」のオンリーワンを目指す中で陶器風呂の開発を進めてきました。それはタヌキを代表する置き物や茶わんや湯飲み、花びんだけではなかなか販売網も広がらず、需要と供給という点でも限界があるからです。信楽の地域でも後継者がなく窯を閉めてしまうところも年々、増えています。この現状を打破し、信楽焼きを全国に、そして海外に広げていくためには新たな挑戦が不可欠でした。

Providing the sense of *wabi-sabi* and warmth unique to ceramics

Interview with Ikuo Muraki, President of Marumoto Seitoh, a manufacturer of *Shigarakiyaki* (ceramic) bathtubs

Q: When I think of *Shigarakiyaki* ceramics, the first thing that comes to mind is an image of a raccoon dog object. They sell Shigarakiyaki raccoon dog items throughout the area, right?

Muraki: Yes. We made our start as a ceramics manufacturer in this part of Shigaraki almost forty years ago. Since that time, we have fully utilized our experience and skill to develop ceramic bathtubs, aiming to create a distinctive appeal that sets us apart as a Shigarakiyaki manufacturer. The reason for this is that raccoon dog items, rice bowls, teacups, and flower vases alone lack the attractive power to expand sales channels. They also have their limits in terms of supply and demand as well. More and more ceramics manufacturers are calling it quits in the Shigaraki area each year because there are not enough people to carry on the business. I felt the inevitable calling to tackle a new challenge and fight this trend so that we can spread the appeal of *Shigarakiyaki* ceramics all over Japan and to countries abroad.

Q: When did you begin making ceramic bathtubs?

Muraki: Being a pioneer in the manufacture of ceramic bathtubs involved a lot of trial and error, but in 1996 we were finally able to begin the full-scale production and sales of ceramic bathtubs. Marumoto Seitoh has delivered more than 4,000 ceramic bathtubs to nearly 1,200 customers so far.

――いつごろから開発に着手されたのですか。

村木　陶器浴槽メーカーの先駆者として試行錯誤を繰り返し、平成八年から本格的に陶器浴槽の製造・販売を開始いたしました。お陰さまで丸元製陶は、これまでに千二百カ所、約四千台以上の陶器浴槽を送りだしております。

——それはすごい実績です。陶器浴槽のポイントは？

村木　特に陶器独特のわびさび、土、そして人のぬくもりを、使っていただく方すべての方々に伝わりますよう努力を重ねていることです。お客さまの使用目的に応じて形や大きさ、風合いもすべてアレンジいたします。まさに手作りですが良質の陶土を使い、これまでのノウハウを生かした制作で求められているものを迅速に作り、納品いたします。最近はどちらかの宿泊施設などで体験された外国人の方がご自宅用に注文したいという声や、銭湯などでも差別化商品として導入されるケースもあります。国内外の方が集まる展示会を中心にアピールしておりますが、本当に全国、国内外問わずご注文いただいている状況です。

——龍名館さんに期待することは？

村木　九室すべてにご注文いただき、納品いたしました。日本の文化を重んじるホテルとお聞きし、信楽焼きの陶器浴槽を通じて日本の陶器文化に触れていただける機会が増えたこと、また当社だけではなく滋賀県甲賀市の信楽に足を運んでいただき、ユニークで愛らしいタヌキの置き物やさまざまな陶器類と出会っていただければと思います。自然に囲まれた地域ですが、全国、そして世界から多くの方が訪れる、そんな活気あふれる街にしていきたいですね。これからも常に改革にチャレンジし、また次世代の技術継承、育成にも注力し、信楽の陶器製品を作り続けていきます。

66

Q: That's a tremendous achievement. What is the distinct appeal of your ceramic bathtubs?

Muraki: The main feature of our production is our consistent efforts to promote the concepts of *wabi-sabi*, earth, and human warmth unique to ceramics to all users. We make delicate arrangements for form, size, and feeling adapted to the way in which the customer uses the product. We use high-quality earth for our handmade products and quickly create and deliver ordered items by fully utilizing the empirical knowledge we have gained through our many years of experience. In recent years, we have received orders from people in other countries who discovered our ceramic bathtubs during their stays at hotels in Japan. These orders include some for home use, along with some from public bath facilities which have installed our bathtubs to give their establishments a distinct appeal. We promote our products mainly through exhibitions where many people from Japan and abroad gather. These exhibitions have brought us many orders from people across Japan and other countries.

Q: What do you expect of Ryumeikan?

Muraki: Ryumeikan graciously called on us to make the bathtubs for all nine rooms of the hotel, and it was an order we were more than happy to handle. The hotel displays great reverence for Japanese culture, and we are grateful they have provided guests with more opportunities to experience Japanese ceramic culture through our *Shigarakiyaki* ceramic bathtubs. I sincerely hope people will come and visit the Shigaraki area in Koka City, Shiga Prefecture and enjoy the unique and pretty raccoon dog objects and many other ceramic items, as well as use our products. Shigaraki is surrounded by a rich natural environment, and I would like to help revitalize the community by attracting as many people as possible to the area from across Japan and around the world. We will continue to tackle the quest for change, and produce *Shigarakiyaki* ceramic items that focus on passing on the art and developing the next-generation of craftsmen.

信楽焼き陶器浴槽　丸元製陶　代表取締役　村木郁夫氏

1964年3月　信楽に生まれる　1982年3月　県立信楽工業高等学校窯業課　卒業　1982年4月　大阪デザイナー専門学院　入学　1984年4月　丸元製陶　入社　1989年10月　専務取締役に就任　2001年10月　代表取締役に就任　現在に至る

Ikuo Muraki, President of Marumoto Seitoh, a manufacturer of Shigarakiyaki bathtubs

Ikuo Muraki was born in Shigaraki in March 1964. He graduated from the ceramic course of Shiga Prefectural Shigaraki High School in March 1982, and then entered Osaka Designers' College in April 1982. He joined Marumoto Seitoh two years later in April 1984. He was appointed Executive Managing Director in October 1989 and President in October 2001, and he has held that post ever since.

畳の構造からヒントを得た積層マットレス

ベッドは畳の上で寝ているような、"日本の伝統的なお布団に近いもの"を探しました。ベッドは高さを低くすることで、日本家屋の畳の部屋のような和の趣を体感できます。

ベッド（マットレス）イワタ
代表取締役社長　岩田有史氏

——ホテルコンセプトに合う国産のベッドマットレスを探した結果、御社のマットレスに行きついたと聞きました。

岩田　当社は百八十年もの永きに渡り、布団づくりを続けてきました。ところが最近では布団の生活からベッドの生活に様式が変化する中で、マットレスのご相談が増えてきたのです。例えば「夏、蒸れて寝苦しい」「スプリングの揺れが気になる」「冬、底冷えがして寒い」このような声を

Multi-layered mattress that draws inspiration from the structure of tatami

We sought a bed that "closely resembles a traditional Japanese futon," one that makes you feel like you are sleeping on a tatami mat. By lowering the height of the bed, we were able to recreate the feeling of lying in a tatami room inside a traditional Japanese house.

Arichika Iwata, President of Iwata Inc., a bed mattress manufacturer

Q: I heard that Ryumeikan discovered your company's mattress in their search for made-in-Japan bed mattresses that fit their concept.

Iwata: We have been manufacturing futons for 180 years. However, over the years we have seen a change in the Japanese lifestyle from futons to beds, and as a result we have received an increasing number of orders for mattresses. People complain about the humidity and discomfort of sleeping in summer, suffering from a shaky feeling in spring, or the cold chill they feel in their bones in the winter. These common complaints from customers motivated us to make our first attempt at producing mattresses. We drew a lot of inspiration from the multi-layered structure of tatami, which in its own right is a Japanese version of a mattress.

Q: Inspiration from the multi-layered structure of tatami?

Iwata: Japanese tatami culture dates back to the Heian period (794-1191). In those days, people used tatami mats in the same way we use mattresses today. They created layers of plant fibers and constructed a perfect structure suitable for Japan's natural environment, creating a cool feel in the summer and warmth in the winter. Japan has four distinct seasons, and the climate, temperature, and humidity vary greatly not only by season, but also by region. Paying special attention to the highly changeable features of Japan's natural environment, we selected the perfect materials to provide a good night's rest to people from across Japan and all around the world. The first thing our staff did was to visit the area where the materials were produced and directly examine the environment, production capability, quality level, and management structure. Next, we analyzed the samples they brought back to the office and conducted a strict examination in accordance with our own stringent criteria. This series of processes—from the assessment of the production environment, procurement, and analysis to the securing of a stable procurement route—enabled us to select safe and reliable materials that form the core essence of bedding. By establishing a base of know-how that brings together the multi-layered structure of tatami, animal hair, such as cashmere, camel, yak, and horse, and a natural luxury material like hemp, we succeeded in producing a new type of mattress in our quest to create a sleeping environment of the utmost comfort.

多数うかがい、当社にとって初めてのマットレス作りに着手したのです。大きなヒントになったのは日本のマットレスとも言うべき「畳」の積層構造でした。

――畳の積層構造からですか？

岩田　畳文化は古くは平安時代に遡り、当時はマットレスのように用いられていました。植物の繊維などを幾層にも重ね、夏は涼しく、冬は暖かくという日本の風土に合った構造を確立していったのです。日本には四季があります。それぞれの季節、また地域によって、気候や温湿度など大きく異なります。そこで当社は変化の激しい日本の風土を考慮し、健やかな睡眠環境に導く最適な素材を、国内外から選び抜きました。まずは現地に赴き、責任者自らの眼で飼育環境・生産環境・品質レベル・管理体制などを検証。その後持ち帰った素材サンプルを分析し、独自の厳しい基準で徹底的に検査します。生産環境の検証・調達・分析・安定した調達ルートの確保―こうした一連の過程を管理することにより、寝具づくりの要である"安心・安全な素材"が選び出されるのです。畳の構造とカシミヤ、キャメル、ヤク、ホースの獣毛、麻の高級天然素材を活かすノウハウを結実させることで、快適な寝心地を追求した新タイプのマットレスを作り出すことができました。

人は通常一晩に10〜20回程度の寝返りをします。寝返りは体の歪みを整えたり、また疲れをとったりするために無意識のうちに行っている体の動きです。つまり寝返りしやすいマットレスが、健康的な眠りには欠かせません。

——ヤクは聞きなれない動物です。どんなところに生息しているのですか。

岩田　モンゴルの奥地や海抜四千ｍ以上の高地など山岳地帯に生息し、遊牧民の暮らしを古くから支えてきた、牛科の動物です。その柔毛は、別名チベットカシミヤともいわれるほど柔らかく繊細です。長毛は、太くて高い支持性があり、身体の沈み込みを防ぎます。保温性・へたりにくさを両立した優れた素材です。動物は生息する場所で生きるための体を作り上げていきます。その効能を融合させることで快眠・安眠を実現できるのです。

——龍名館に期待することは。

岩田　龍名館さんは本当にお客さまのことを大切に思われています。また和食などの食文化だけではなく、このマットレスを通じて日本古来の生活文化を海外の方に体感していただけることは素晴らしいことです。一人でも多くの方に体感していただきたいですね。

The average person turns over in bed ten to twenty times at night while sleeping. Turning over in bed is an unconscious movement people do when they are sleeping to correct physical distortion or alleviate exhaustion. This means that a mattress on which people can turn over more easily is essential for healthy sleep.

Q: The yak is an animal we don't hear often. What kind of habitat do they live in?

Iwata: Yaks live in mountainous areas, such as the hinterlands of Mongolia and highlands more than 4,000 meters above sea level. They belong to the same family of animals as cows and have long supported the livelihood of nomadic people. Their extremely soft and delicate hair is sometimes referred to as Tibetan cashmere. This hair is also extremely long and thick, making it able to firmly support the body of a person sleeping on a bed and prevent the body from sinking. As a material, yak hair retains heat well and is incredibly sturdy. The characteristics of yak hair reflect the physical features animals develop to survive in their habitats. By making the most of these features, we succeeded in creating a mattress perfect for a comfortable and secure night's sleep.

Q: What do you expect of Ryumeikan?

Iwata: Ryumeikan demonstrates the utmost consideration for its guests. In addition, I think it's truly wonderful that the hotel provides guests from other countries with the opportunity to experience traditional Japanese lifestyle and culture through our mattresses, along with food culture, such as Japanese cuisine. I sincerely hope we can help deliver this kind of experience to as many people as possible.

Arichika Iwata, President of Iwata Inc., a bed mattress manufacturer

Arichika Iwata is President of Iwata Inc. He is active in the provision of consulting services for sleep environments and habits, educational training programs on sleep, the development of sleep-related products, the development of bedding, and the training of sleep environment advisors. He acts as a bridge between sleep research institutes and business.

ベッド（マットレス）イワタ　代表取締役社長　株式会社イワタ　代表取締役社長　岩田有史氏　睡眠環境、睡眠習慣のコンサルティング、眠りに関する教育研修、睡眠関連商品の開発、寝具の開発、睡眠環境アドバイザーの育成、などを行っている。睡眠研究機関と産業を繋ぐ橋渡し役として活躍する。

東京・八重洲の「ホテル龍名館東京」同様、「ホテル龍名館お茶の水本店」もアメニティにこだわりました。洗面スペースには、風呂敷でアメニティをご用意。風呂敷はどんな形のものでも自由自在にくるむことができる日本人の知恵で生まれたものです。風呂敷は繊細でありながら、とても機能的で、何度も使え、日本人のエコの精神が宿っています。アメニティは女性の皆さまにもご満足いただけるよう豊富にご用意。私たちはむやみに新しいものを取り入れることはもはや流行遅れであり、いかに物を大切にしながら運営できるかが現代のホテルにおいて求められていると考えたのです。

Hotel Ryumeikan Ochanomizu Honten paid special attention to amenities, just like Hotel Ryumeikan Tokyo near the Yaesu Entrance of Tokyo Station. We provided amenity sets wrapped in a *furoshiki* (Japanese wrapping cloth) in the washroom of each room. A *furoshiki* is handy for wrapping things of all different shapes, and is a good example of an item created by Japanese ingenuity. Though it is rather delicate, a *furoshiki* is a highly functional item made to withstand the rigors of repeated use, a trademark of Japan's ecological mindset. We provide a rich set of amenities especially intended for the delight of female guests. In terms of management, we believe that contemporary hotels have an obligation to afford these things great care and affection. Hotels today can no longer introduce new things without giving them much thought.

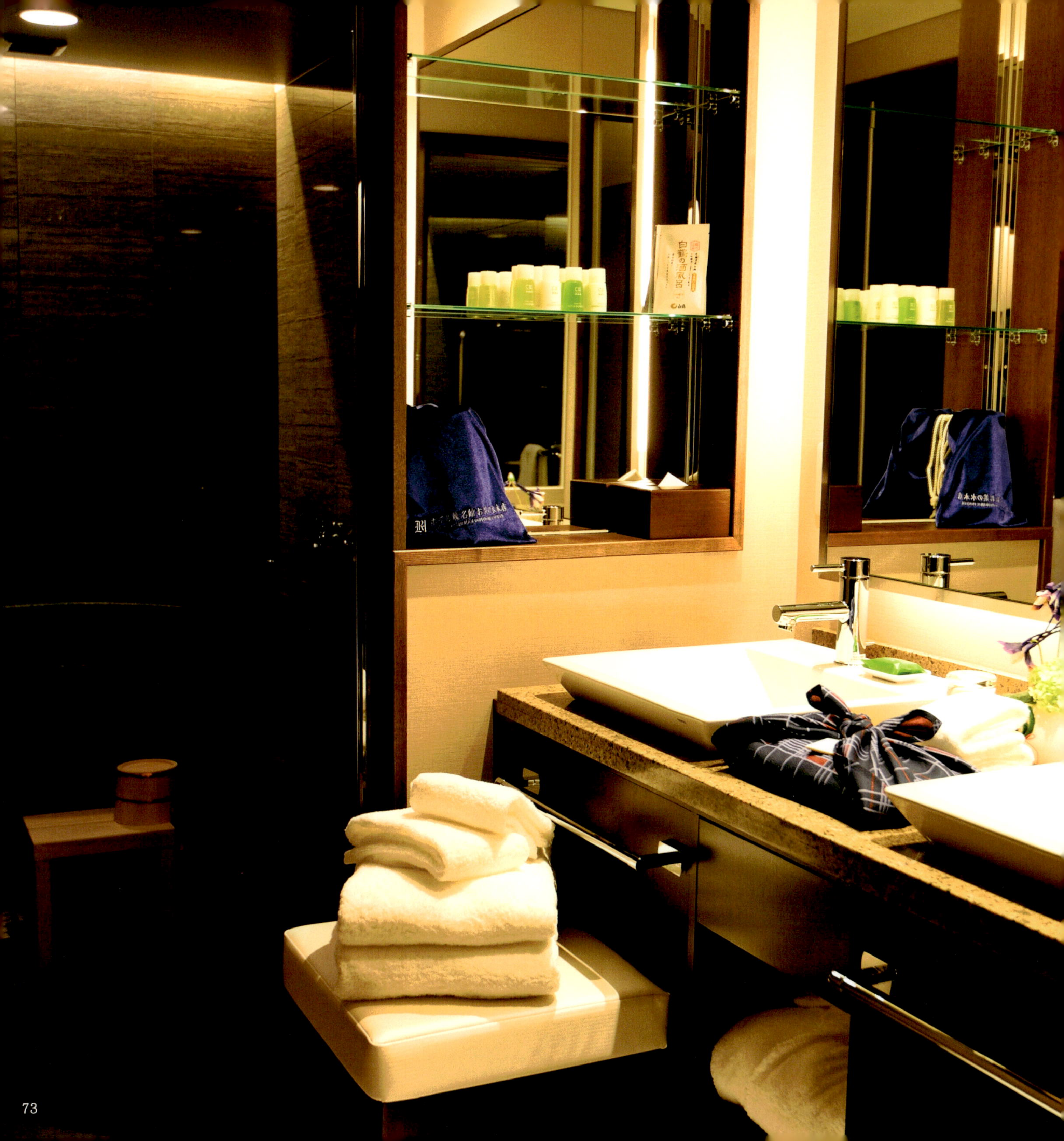
白鶴の酒風呂

日本のエコロジーの考え方は江戸時代にさかのぼります。「知足　足(たる)を知る」遺教経に「若し諸の苦悩を脱せんと欲せば、まさに知足を観ずべし。知足の法はすなわち富楽安穏の処なり。知足の人は地上に臥すといえども、安楽なりとなす。不知足の者は富むといえども、しかも貧し。知足の者は常に五欲のために牽かれて、知足の者のために憐憫せらる。是を知足と名づく」とあるそうです。つまり貧乏とは何も持っていない人のことでなく、多くを持ちながらまだまだ欲しいと満足できない人。足を知るということは欲望が制御され、煩悩妄想による迷いもおのずと消え、心清き状態であることを指しています。引き出しを開けるとそこには日本の伝統の遊びである「折り紙」をご用意。折り方については、ぜひスタッフにお尋ねください。引き出しに収納することや風呂敷に包むということは、日本人の知恵で生まれた繊細な文化の一つなのです。

The ecological mindset of Japanese people dates back to the Edo period (1603-1867). There is a Buddhist sutra that emphasizes the significance of knowing the true meaning of contentment. In short, the sutra claims the impoverished are not those with nothing, but those who already have a lot but cannot be satisfied with all that they have. Those who understand what it means to be content have a pure heart free from being distracted and controlled by earthly desires. With this in mind, we provide *origami*, a traditional Japanese folding paper, in the drawer of each guest room. Please feel free to ask our staff for paper-folding tips. Placing objects in drawers and wrapping items in *furoshiki* are just two examples of subtle and delicate forms of culture created by Japanese ingenuity.

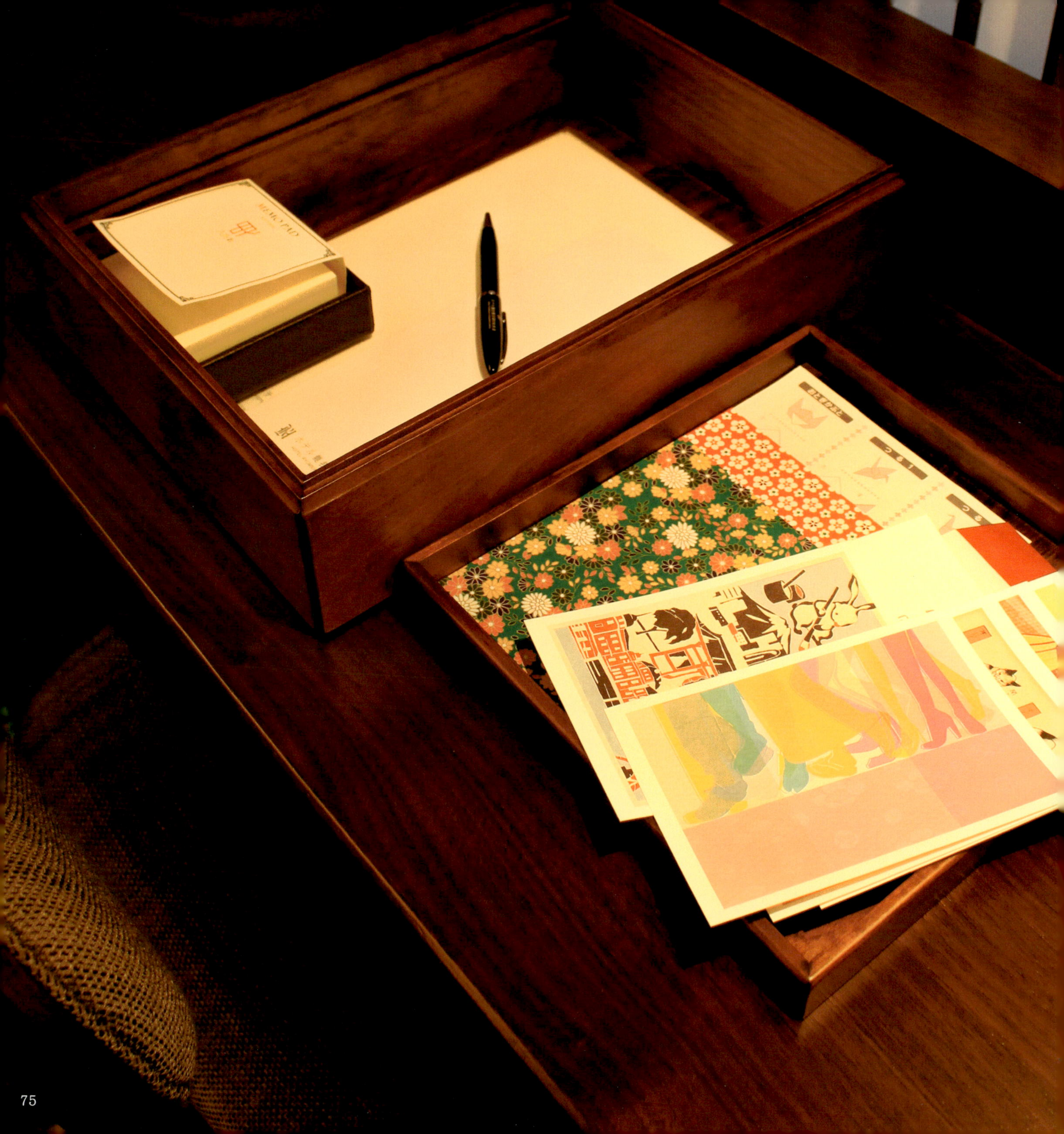

ご朝食は旅館の感覚を味わっていただけますようお部屋でお召し上がりいただけます。また、1階レストランでも開放的なテラス席で神田・お茶の水の静かな朝の時間をお過ごしいただけます。お帰りの際は、ぜひトラベルノートに旅の思い出を記していってください。これからの百年も変わらずこの地で、このトラベルノートとともに、お客さまをお待ちしております。またいつでもお越しください。

You can eat breakfast in your room and enjoy the original atmosphere of a ryokan. You can also enjoy a quiet morning in the Kanda-Ochanomizu area from a seat in the open terrace of the restaurant on the first floor. When you check out, we encourage you to write about your trip in our travel notebook. This travel notebook is a testament to the guests we have served, and will continue to be so as we welcome guests to this area for the next 100 years. Please feel free to visit us again at any time.

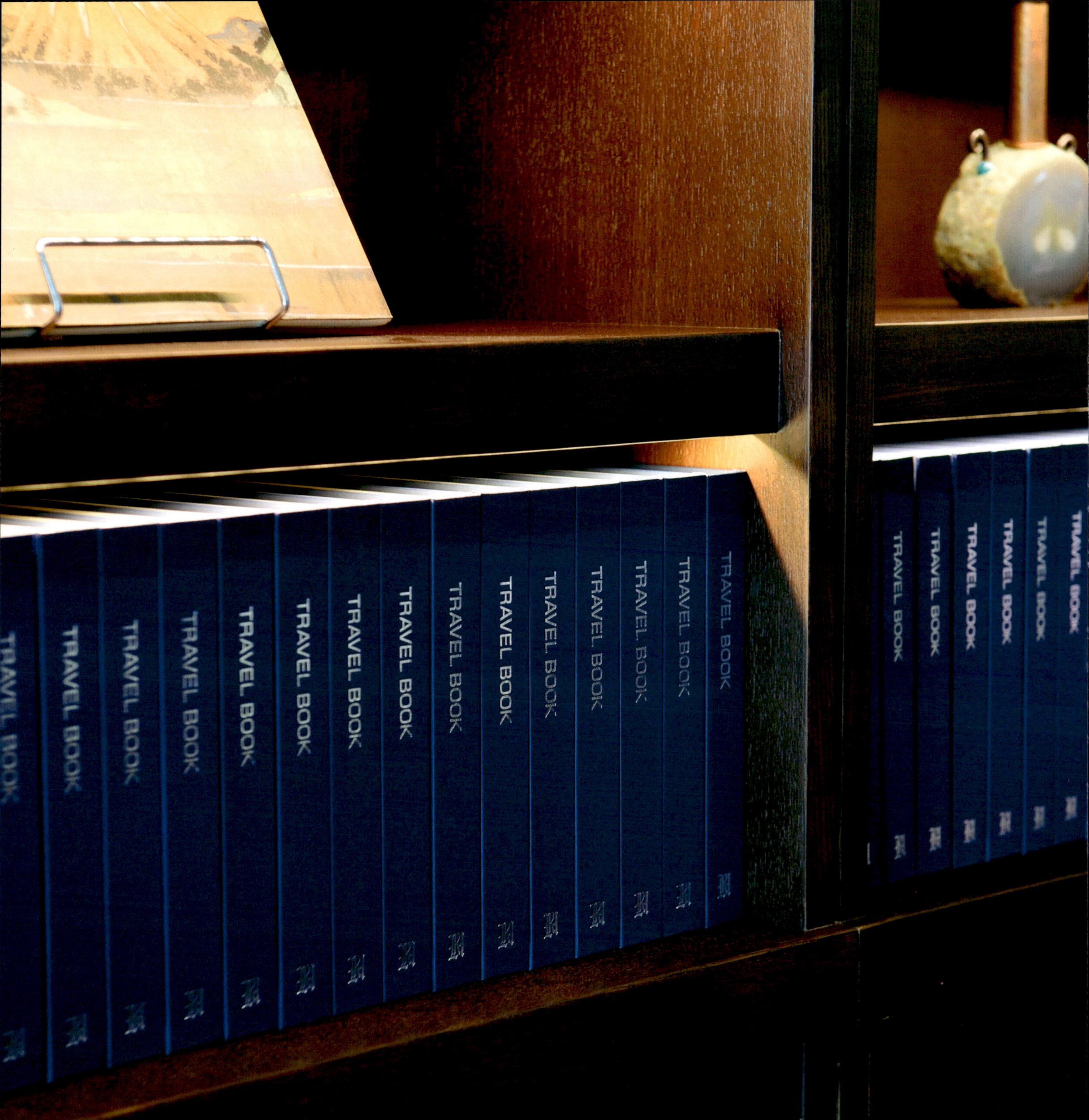
TRAVEL BOOK

古来の美と
斬新な用と美に
包まれた空間で
心ゆくまで

アートディレクター
イデアルデザインアンドプロダクト　大良隆司氏

――まず始めに、今回のリニューアルにおけるインテリアコンセプトは？

大良　キャッチコピーは「古来の美と斬新な用と美に包まれた空間で、心ゆくまでおくつろぎください」です。伝統的な日本の色や創業当時の帳場の障子をインテリアとして再現するなど繊細でわびさびを感じさせる美しさを持ちつつも、古都・京都にないような先進性や都会的な要素と共存した空間、インテリアを作り出すことです。東京の旅館では稀有な陶器風呂や茶の湯を髣髴させる江戸の伝統色である群青色（ぐんじょういろ）の水紋柄カーペットを見立て、また和空間の直線的な構成に有機的デザインのイスを備えた空間でなごみを感じていただけるようにしました。清らかな心で都心の時間を過ごせること、陰翳礼讃の美を追求しました。

Relaxing to your heart's content in a space that combines old beauty with innovative functionality and beauty.

Art Director Takashi Taira of Ideal Design & Product

Q: What was your interior concept behind the recent hotel renewal project?
Taira: My catchphrase was "relaxing to your heart's content in a space that combines old beauty with innovative functionality and beauty." Basically, this means creating a space and interior that harmoniously coexists with sophisticated urban elements not seen in Kyoto, the old capital of Japan, and the beauty of *wabi-sabi* with all of its subtleties. We achieved this by reproducing traditional Japanese colors and incorporating the *shoji* (traditional Japanese sliding paper door) used at the reception desk around the time the hotel was founded. I designed a ceramic bathtub, something rather unique for a ryokan in Tokyo, and a water ring-patterned carpet of lapis lazuli, a traditional color of Edo that conjures up images of the tea ceremony. I also created a relaxing atmosphere in a space featuring linear Japanese-style architecture, complete with chairs of an organic design. I sought to help guests spending time in an urban setting achieve a pure state of mind and accentuate the beauty found in appreciating shadows.

Q: What particular approach did you take for all of the guest rooms?
Taira: I designed guest rooms that seek to create a space for guests to experience Japanese-style material and sense. Japanese beauty consists of fine and delicate vertical lines. These lines produce a harmonious yet confined atmosphere that encompasses the entire space, while at the same time creating a Japanese feeling. It was essential to simulate the feeling of relaxing in a place that was part hotel, part home. This feeling would better enable guests to appreciate objects of beauty and coexist with them by directly feeling and experiencing the beauty they produce. To this end, I designed guest rooms that combine elements of both slight tension and relaxation by introducing round-shaped sofas and *Shigarakiyaki* ceramic bathtubs that evoke a feeling of warmth.

Q: How about the restaurant?
Taira: The restaurant's concept was "having tea-themed dishes," so I introduced tea-related color coordinates, choosing a light brown "Edo tea," a yellow "Rikyu tea," the color that is said to have been the favorite of tea master Sen No Rikyu, and a soft yellowish green "green tea" for the furniture of the restaurant. I also installed a unique lighting system to simulate the atmosphere of the tea ceremony.

―客室全体にはどのようなことを工夫されましたか。

大良　客室は和の素材と趣を体感する空間であることをベースに発展させました。日本の美はきめ細かな繊細な縦線です。縦線は空間全体を引き締め、また和の趣を醸し出させます。しかし体感するという意味で美しいものを眺める、美しいものと自身を共存させるためには、ホテルと住宅の中間的なリラックス感が欠かせません。そこであえてラウンド型のソファを導入したり、ぬくもりを感じさせる信楽焼きの陶器風呂を導入したり、緊張感とゆるみのある客室を作りました。

―レストランにおいてはいかがですか？

大良　"茶を食す"ことをテーマとしたレストランでしたので、薄い茶色の染め色である「江戸茶」や茶人・千利休好みの黄色と言われている「利休茶」、また抹茶のようなやわらかい黄緑の「抹茶色」をレストランの家具に使うなど、お茶にちなんだ風合いでコーディネートしました。また茶の湯を表現した個性的な照明も設置しました。

—今回のリニューアルプロジェクトに関われていかがでしたか。

大良　次世代に継承していきたいという龍名館さんの社長はじめ、スタッフの方々の前向きな気持ち、そして真剣に取り組む姿勢はとても感激しました。普通であれば人任せで終わってしまうのですが、僕たちが、私たちが次の世代のホテルを作るんだという意識はとても高く、意見や考えの相違などがあり、白熱することもありました。しかしながら、プロデューサーの芹沢さんを仲介役にお互いが理解し、本当に納得のできる空間、インテリアデザインができたことに感謝し、満足しています。近代的な高層タワーの横に鳥居や地蔵があるという、東京ならではの和の在り方、そして開発テーマである"学ぶ"を見つけ出せる九室二フロアのホテル、いや旅館として、また新たな一歩を歩き出せたこと、またそこに関われたことに感謝申し上げます。

アートディレクター　イデアルデザインアンドプロダクト　大良隆司氏
1968年北海道生まれ。生家は家具建具製作所を営んでいた。国内家具メーカーでプロダクトデザイナーを経たのち、外資系デザイン事務所へ。海外デザイナーとのデザインコラボレーションの中で、あらためて日本の伝統美に触れる。以後、東洋美と西洋美の出逢いをテーマに、ホテル空間を中心としたデザインプロデュースを手掛ける。

Ryumeikan to take a new step forward as a ryokan with nine guest rooms and two floors, offering people spaces where they can discover the concept of "learning" that drove the project's development.

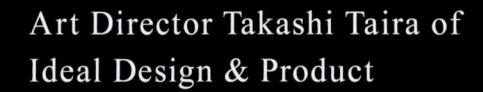

Art Director Takashi Taira of Ideal Design & Product

Takashi Taira was born in Hokkaido in 1968. His family ran a furniture and construction material manufacturing business. After working as a product designer for domestic furniture manufacturers, he moved to a design office run by a foreign company. He rediscovered traditional Japanese aesthetics through collaborative design work with designers from other countries. He eventually became involved in producing designs mainly for hotel spaces that focus on the fusion of Eastern and Western art.

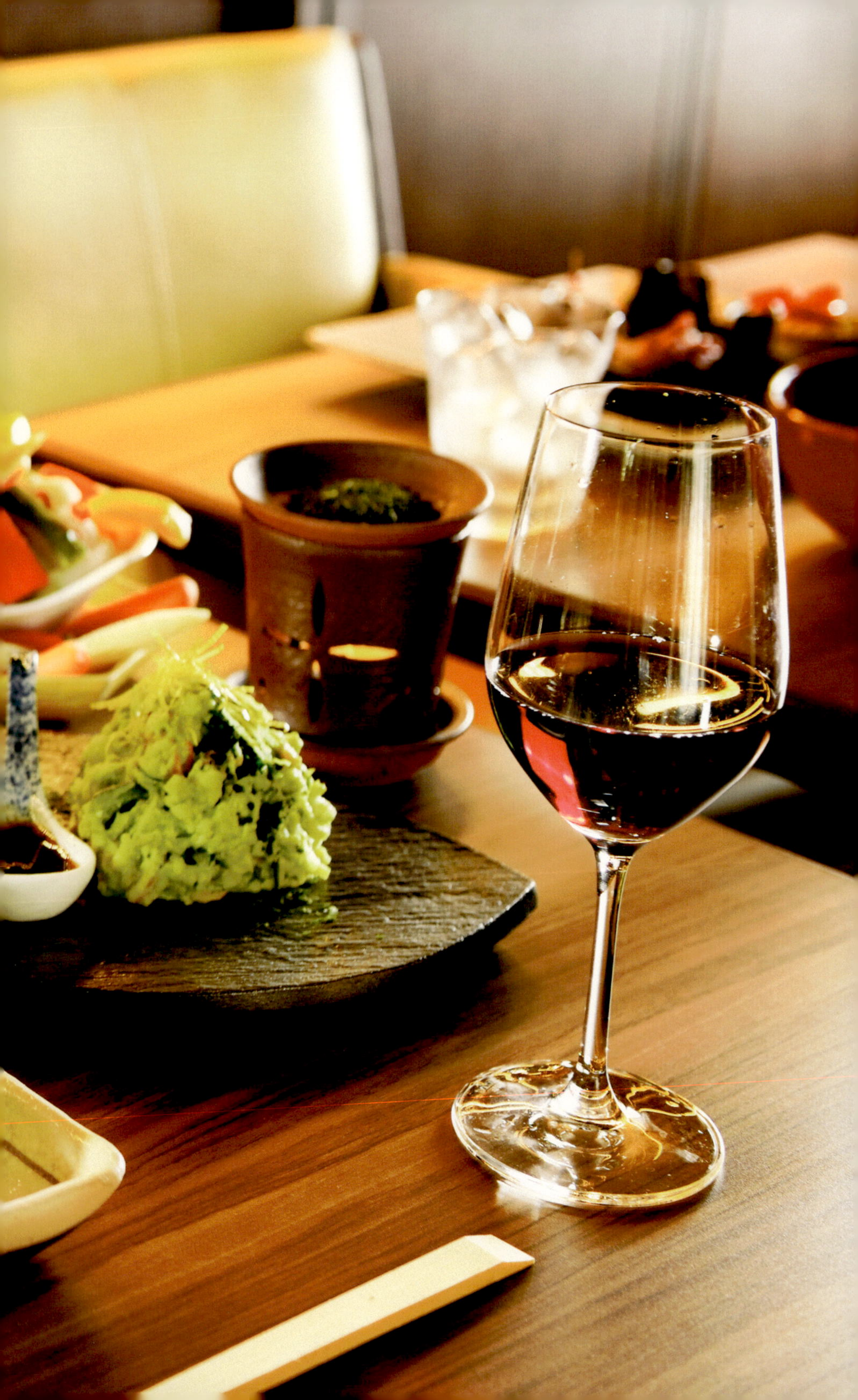

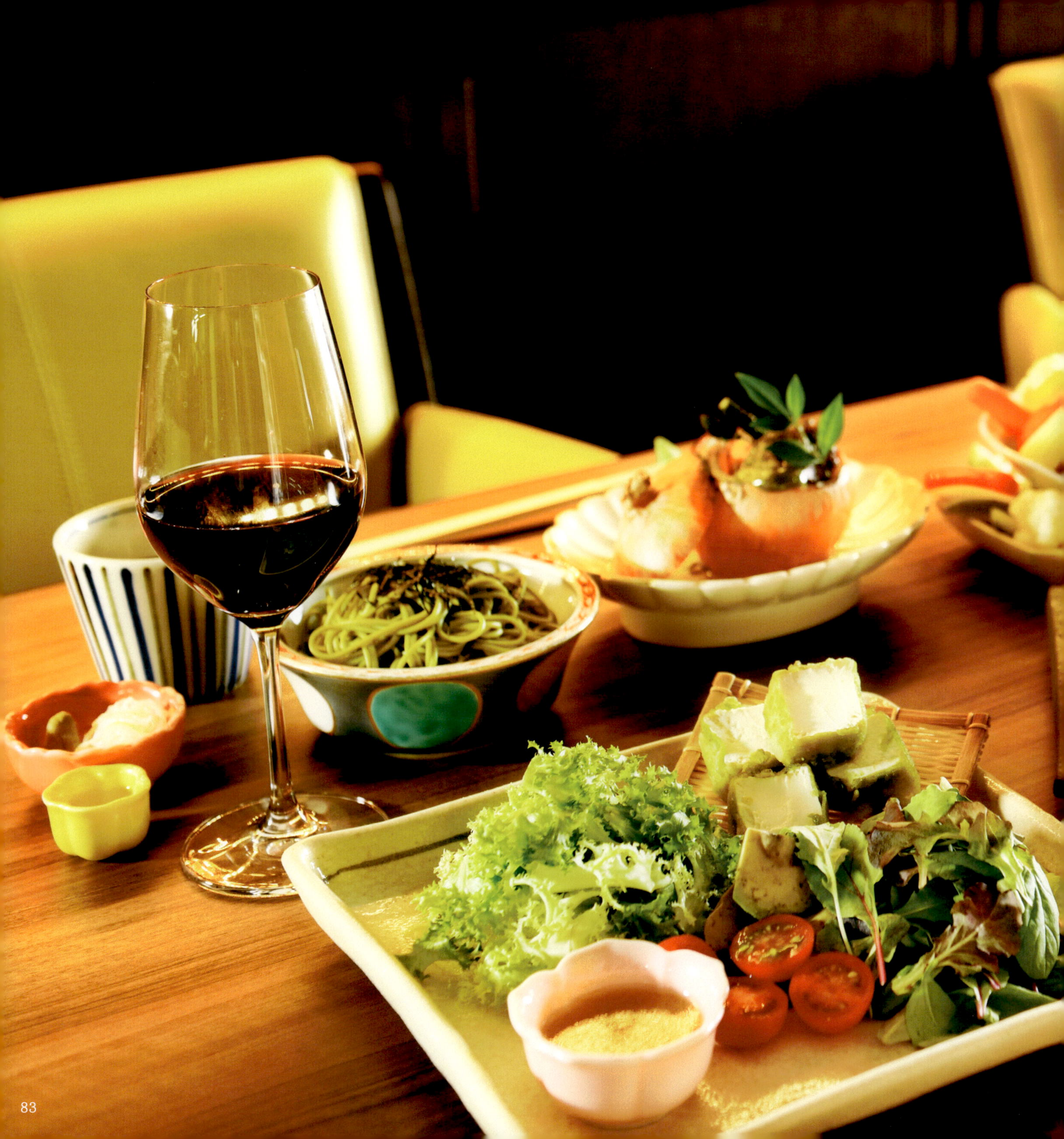

GREEN TEA
RESTAURANT
1899
OCHANOMIZU

85

86

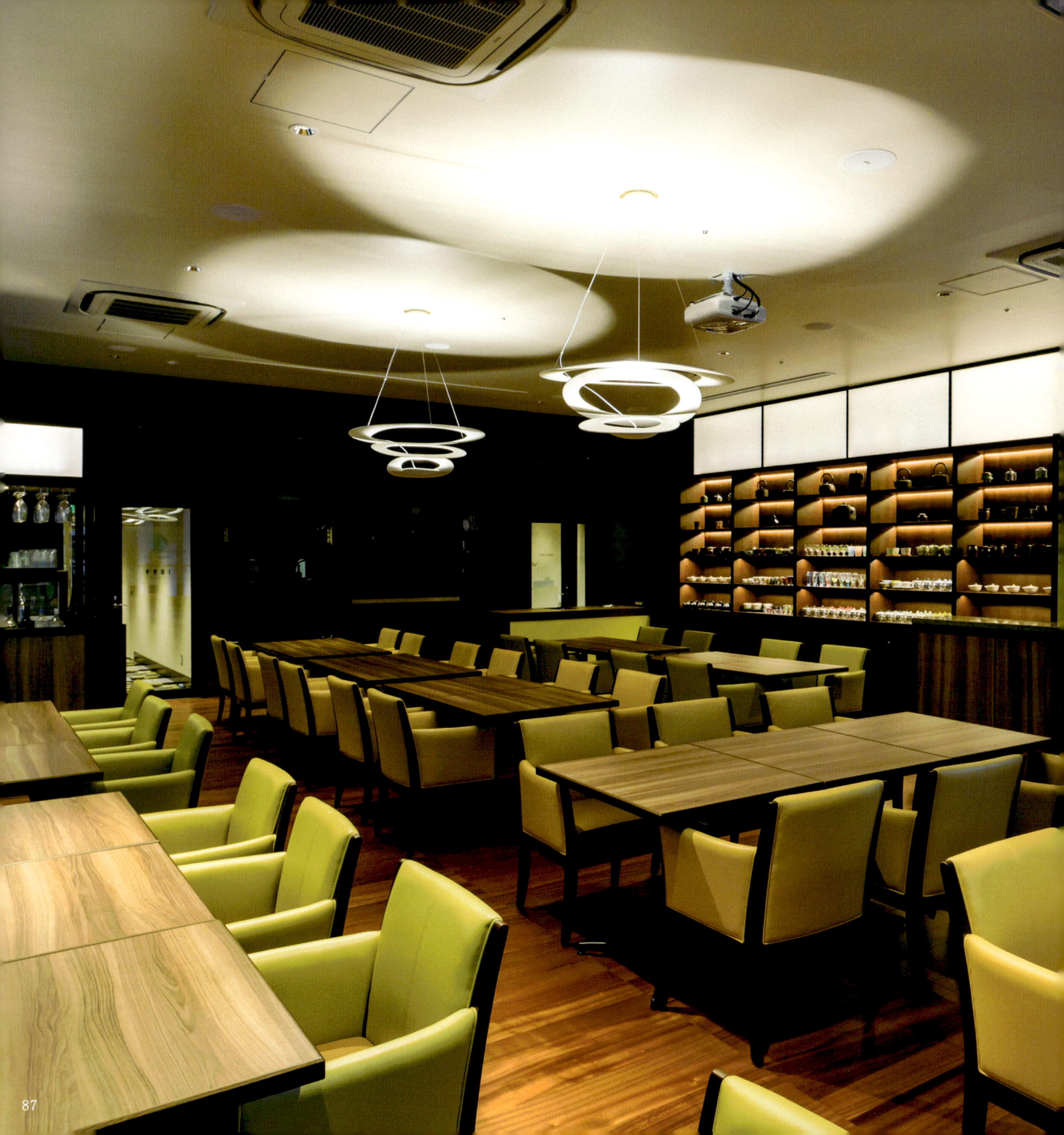

[GREEN TEA RESTAURANT 1899 OCHANOMIZU]は若い世代を中心に薄れ始めている日本茶の文化を、龍名館なりに発信していきたいと考えています。お茶のあるおもてなしの食風景を創るレストランです。お茶そのものは海外や栄養学の面で注目されていますが、ペットボトルの普及により急須で日本茶を淹れる文化が薄れ始めています。そんな中、新たな日本茶の提案や、啓蒙活動が見られるようになってきました。幸いにお茶の水は過去に徳川家に献上するお茶用の水が湧き出ていたことに由来され、お茶との関係が深い地域でした。そこで改めて地域に愛される店舗を目指して、龍名館の創業年数を刻み、店舗名を[GREEN TEA RESTAURANT 1899 OCHANOMIZU]としました。お茶を飲むだけでなく、龍名館が創業時から大切にしてきた和食とお茶を組み合わせて新しい和食の在り方を提案することを目指しています。

Chapter 4: Aiming to offer "dining and tea steeped with hospitality"

Ryumeikan seeks to disseminate the culture of Japanese tea that is becoming less popular among young people through its Green Tea Restaurant 1899 Ochanomizu. The aim of this restaurant is to offer dining and tea steeped with hospitality. Tea itself attracts a lot interest from people abroad and in terms of its nutritional benefits, but widespread use of pet bottles is causing the traditional culture of making Japanese tea in a *kyusu* (small teapot) to fade away. In the midst of this trend, we now see a wave of new proposals for enjoying Japanese tea and various awareness-raising campaigns. Fortunately for Ryumeikan, the name Ochanomizu comes from area's history of providing the Tokugawa shogunate with spring water during the Edo period (1603-1867). As this clearly demonstrates, Ochanomizu is closely associated with tea, and that is why we included the year Ryumeikan was founded within the restaurant name and named it Green Tea Restaurant 1899 Ochanomizu. The name also reflects our renewed determination to be an establishment cherished by local communities. In addition to enjoying tea, we aim to propose a new type of Japanese dining experience by bringing together Japanese food and tea, two things Ryumeikan has focused on since it began business.

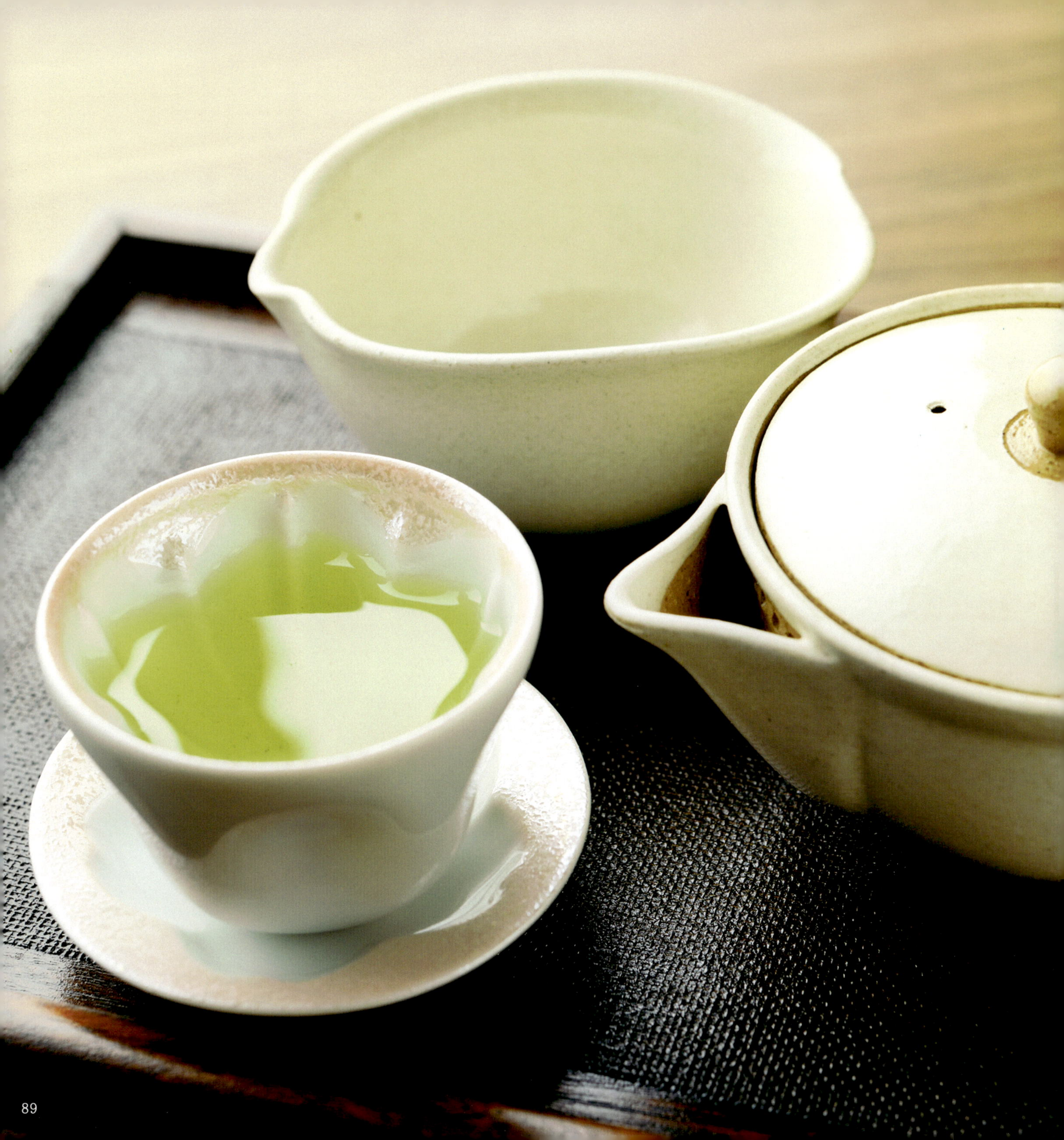

お茶のソムリエである「茶バリエ」はお茶の文化の発信、伝えられるコミュニケーションを持つこと、専門性として資格取得の奨励も行い、お客さまに日本茶の素晴らしさを伝えていきます。素材の茶葉は専門家とともに厳選し、水は茶釜にて十分に沸騰させた軟水を使用しています。またさらにお茶の魅力を感じていただくため、店内では、さまざまな湯呑茶碗をディスプレイしお好みの茶碗をお選びいただけます。めずらしい茶碗もご用意。茶碗を含め、和紙や小物もお茶のあるおもてなしの食風景に欠かせないアイテムです。茶バリエが淹れる香り高い一杯を味わえるのはもちろん、料理やスイーツで"茶を食す"楽しさをご用意しました。

The "*chabarie,*" or tea sommelier, is devoted to promoting tea culture and the wonderful charm of Japanese tea to guests. The *chabarie* at our restaurant are encouraged to hone their communication skills and become certified tea specialists. We select high-quality tea leaves based on expert advice and use soft water fully boiled in a teakettle. In addition, we display a variety of tea cups in the store, including rare ones, so that guests can enjoy the appeal of tea and choose a cup that fits their preferences. In addition to tea cups, *washi* (traditional Japanese paper) and accessories are also essential items for dining and tea steeped with hospitality. We provide guests with a cup of exquisitely flavored tea made by our *chabarie*, enabling them to experience the pleasure of "having tea" with delicious dishes and sweets.

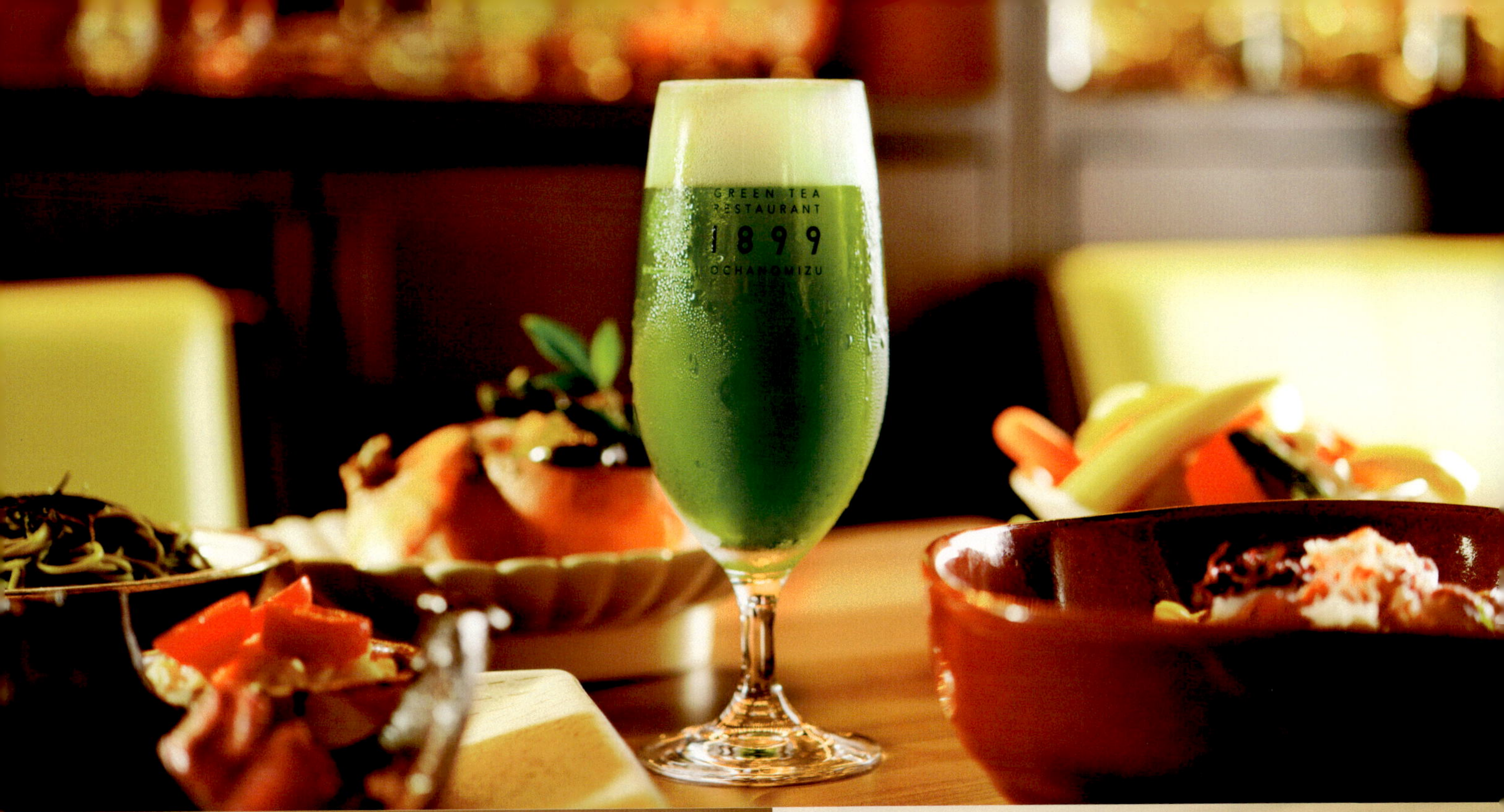
GREEN TEA
RESTAURANT
1899
OCHANOMIZU

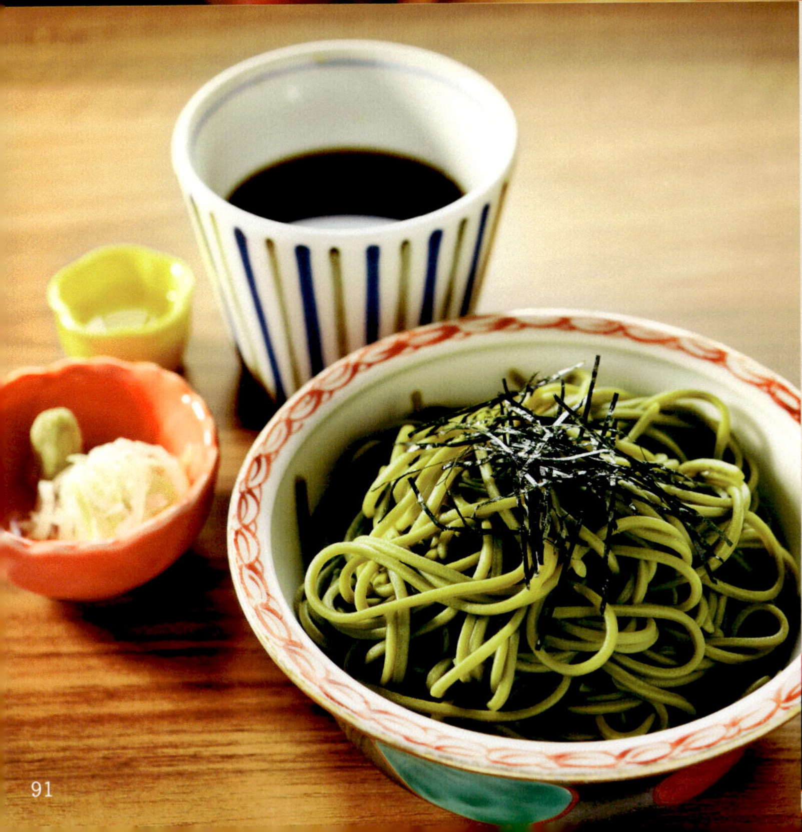

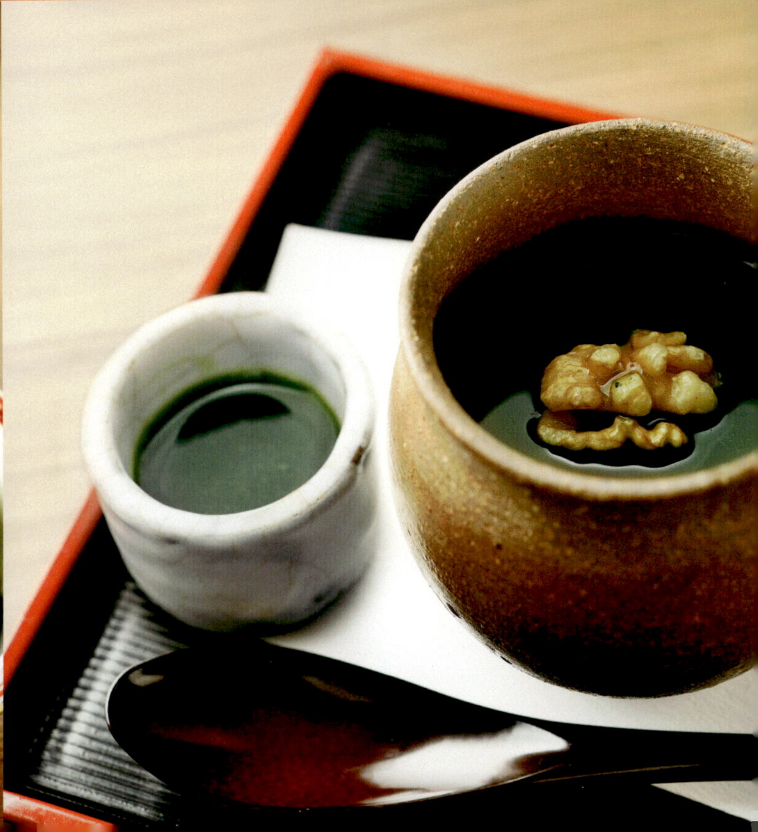

時代に
合わせた
お茶の料理を
発信したい

料理長　大久保将史

—お茶をテーマとしたレストランの料理長として最もポイントとしていることは？

大久保　お茶の可能性をより多くの方に知っていただくことです。私自身、専門学校卒業後、日本料理の世界で修業を積んできました。今回、お茶をテーマとしたレストランの料理長となり、初めてお茶と向き合いました。もちろん、調理の過程ではお茶の葉を使うことはありました。ところがお茶そのものを題材にや食材を柔らかく仕上げると言う点で欠かせないものでした。臭み消し料理することは初の試みでした。

—どのように開発されてきたのですか。

大久保　まずはこれまでの経験や、資料を研究したり、師匠にも助言をいただきました。また、先輩たちにも聞いてみたりしましたがなかなか見出せませんでした。そんなあるとき、お茶料理は三百年以上前から存在し、長い歴史のある伝統的な日本料理であることに気付いたのです。しかし、お茶を淹れる文化が薄れていくに合せてお茶料理も馴染みのない方が多いのが現状です。日本料理を続けてきた料理人として、時代に合わせたお茶料理を通して、その魅力を発信していきたいと思っています。

Desire to promote tea dishes in tune with the tastes of the times.

Interview with Executive Chef Masafumi Okubo

Q: What is your main focus as the executive chef of a restaurant centered around tea?

Okubo: My primary focus is presenting the possibilities of tea to as many people as possible. I developed my skills in the field of Japanese cuisine after graduating from a vocational school. When I was appointed as the executive chef of a restaurant centered around tea, it was the first time I ever had to seriously think about tea. Of course, I had used tea leaves for cooking before I took charge of the tea restaurant. Tea leaves are indispensable for removing smell and cooking foods in a way that softens them up. But it was my first experience preparing dishes centered around tea itself.

Q: How did you develop the dishes you serve?

Okubo: The first thing I did was go back over my past experience. I worked on different ingredients and consulted my head teacher. I also asked my predecessors for advice, but was unable to gain a clear image. Then, suddenly one day I realized that tea-themed cuisine was essentially a traditional form of Japanese cuisine with a long history of more than 300 years. However, today the culture of making tea is no longer widely practiced, and people have become less familiar with tea dishes. As a Japanese cuisine chef, I want to spread the appeal of tea dishes by providing items that match the tastes of the present era.

大久保　この お茶の力の地で、お茶の料理を発信し、自身かれ茶料理の新しい歴史を築いていきたいと考えています。調べていくとお茶は奥深く、茶葉といってもそうとうな種類があります。また、健康志向が強まる中で、本当に必要な日本伝統の食材ということがわかり始めてきました。

――はい。どうしてもお茶は飲むという印象が強く、食べるとしても抹茶アイスやケーキなど、粉末の抹茶を使ったスイーツが中心となってしまいます。

大久保　そうですね。なかなかお茶そのものを食べるという感覚は少ないと思います。ほうじ茶で炊いた茶飯や、抹茶を使った料理、また煎茶に浸した「茶油」を作り、お茶を使った料理のアイデアは尽きません。それを考え、試作を繰り返し、メニューとして提供できることは料理人としての喜びです。ぜひ「1899の料理を楽しんでください。先人たちが培ってきたものをアレンジすることでお茶の素晴らしさ、日本のお茶文化への気づきにつながることを使った料理を日々、考える中で多くのアイデアが生まれてきます。煎茶に浸した「茶油」を作り、お茶を使った料理のアイデアは尽きません。それを考え、試作を繰り返し、メニューとして提供できることは料理人としての喜びです。ぜひ「1899の料理を楽しんでください。先人たちが培ってきたものをアレンジすることでお茶の素晴らしさ、日本のお茶文化への気づきにつながることを願います。

GREEN TEA RESTAURANT 1899 OCHANOMIZU　料理長　大久保将史

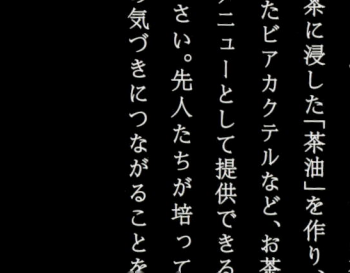

埼玉県出身。武蔵野調理師専門学校卒業。都内は六本木、上野、八重洲の日本料理、河豚専門店で修業し、その後㈱龍名館に入社。二〇一四年、東京都中央区の『花ごよみ東京』の料理長を務める。同年八月一日、GREEN TEA RESTAURANT 1899 OCHANOMIZUの立ち上げとともに料理長に就任。「日本茶のあるおもてなしの食風景」を創り上げるため、従来の「お茶は飲み物」という概念とは一線を画した、新たな和食の在り方を模索している。店舗での真摯な料理作りに取り組む

料理長〉は、オフタイムで見せるユーモアの溢れた「お茶目」な二つの顔を持つ。

Q: Sounds like you have the right approach.

Okubo: I want to build a new history of tea-themed cuisine by promoting tea dishes here in Ochanomizu. As I dug deeper into tea, I discovered that tea has an immense world all of its own, and that tea leaves come in all sorts of types. In addition, the growing trend of health-conscious eating helped me to gradually realize that tea is a really an essential part of traditional Japanese food.

Q: That's right. Many people tend to think that tea is something they should drink. Even when they think of having tea dishes, they often gravitate towards sweets that feature green tea-based ingredients, such as green tea ice cream and green tea cake.

Okubo: I agree. I feel many people are unaccustomed to the idea of just enjoying tea on its own. But in thinking about tea dishes every day, I come up with lots of ideas. For example, I made a kind of "tea oil" by mixing tea with oil and using it for cooking. I have numerous ideas about tea dishes, such as rice cooked with toasted tea, tea-based dishes, and beer cocktails. It's a lot of fun as a cook to put these ideas into action, test them out, and then serve them as menu items. I sincerely hope that guests enjoy the dishes we prepare at Green Tea Restaurant 1899 Ochanomizu. I also hope that in making novel arrangements of ideas developed by those before us, we will rediscover the distinct appeal of tea and Japanese tea culture.

Masafumi Okubo, Executive Chef of Green Tea Restaurant 1899 Ochanomizu

Masafumi Okubo was born in Saitama Prefecture, and is a graduate of Musashino Cooking College. He joined Ryumeikan after working as a trainee at Japanese restaurants and blowfish restaurants in Roppongi, Ueno, and Yaesu. He worked as the chef of Hanagoyomi Tokyo in Chuo Ward in 2014, and was appointed as the executive chef of Green Tea Restaurant 1899 Ochanomizu on August 1, 2014, the day the restaurant opened for business. To deliver "dining and Japanese tea steeped with hospitality," he aims to develop a new type of Japanese cuisine that breaks away from the conventional perception of tea as merely something to drink. There are two different sides to Mr. Okubo, one being the "executive chef" seriously devoted to preparing *ocha* (tea) dishes in a restaurant kitchen, the other being the "*ochame* (playful)" individual quick to flash his good sense of humor when he's not working in the kitchen.

この石は木造時代の旅館龍名館本店の玄関前と中庭にオブジェとして置いていたものです。下の写真の石は「GREEN TEA RESTAURANT 1899 OCHANOMIZU」の店頭にあるもう一つの石とセットで、雨が降ると、二つの石の間を、まるで川が流れるように水がたまったそうです。中庭に描いた日本ならではの風情を演出していました。

This stone was placed at the entrance of Ryumeikan's head building, and in its courtyard when the hotel was still a wooden ryokan. The stone in the photograph in the bottom right is set with another stone and placed in the Green Tea Restaurant 1899 Ochanomizu. When it rains, the water is said to well up and seemingly form a river running between the two stones. These stones help create a Japanese-style atmosphere in the courtyard.

Closing words

My initial encounter with Ryumeikan was through a report I did on it for *Hoteres*, a weekly journal on the hotel and restaurant industry. I was impressed by their persistence in overcoming the many difficulties and challenges of running their daily operations. I was consumed by an irrepressible desire to introduce the hotel to readers, and asked Ryumeikan to accept my proposal to write a series of articles about the hotel. I wrote a one-year serial story titled *"Ichigan-zokuso (Running on in Close Unity)."* In covering Ryumeikan for this story, I was struck with the toughness with which this hotel, despite being a small establishment, had endured for more than 100 years together with the local community and its guests, continuing to thrive to this day. The up-and-coming generation of staff in their twenties and thirties exhibit a sense of unity that extends beyond the bounds of their respective operational sections. Moved and touched by their solidarity, the maintenance and cleaning service providers are also dedicated to doing their part as Ryumeikan staff to offer guests safe and comfortable rooms where they can enjoy a good night's sleep. I was so impressed by their well-orchestrated efforts that I came up with the phrase *"ichigan-zokuso (running on in close unity),"* and ultimately used it as the title of my story. Hotel Ryumeikan Ochanomizu Honten reopened with only nine guest rooms in the summer of 2014. This renewal is the culmination of their essential passion for passing on the first-generation head's policy of remaining true to their roots as a Japanese-style inn (ryokan) to the next generation. They created traditional Japanese designs for the many different spaces, such as the *Shigarakiyaki* (pottery) bathtub and Japanese-style front door and carpet. The sense of expression in these spaces is reserved, natural, and modest. They make me feel as if I am being welcomed with the warm hospitality of an old Japanese home, and harken back to the Japanese sentiments of the days of yore. Through this book, I have striven to express the desire to convey to the next generation the tradition of Ryumeikan, one that is founded upon over 100 years of history of serving guests and always giving them the consideration the deserve.

Corporate officer Hirono Yamashita of Ohta Publications Co., Ltd.

おわりに

龍名館との出会いはホテル・レストラン向け業界専門誌「週刊ホテルレストラン」の取材だった。常に走りながらさまざまな困難や問題を乗り越えている姿に感動し、ぜひ読者に聞かせたいと思い連載を依頼、「一丸続走（いちがんぞくそう）」のタイトルで一年間綴った。取材を続けるほどに小粒ながらも百年を超える歳月を地域とともに、お客さまとともに歩み、そして今もなお歩み続けているたくましさを感じた。しかも次世代をとなる二十代、三十代のスタッフがそれぞれの業務を越えて一丸となり取り組んでいる。その姿にメンテナンスや客室清掃会社も心打たれ、龍名館のスタッフの一員として、安全・快適・快眠できる客室の提供に取り組んでいる。まさに一丸となり走り続けている一丸続走であることを確信した。二〇一四年夏、たった九室の「ホテル龍名館お茶の水本店」が装いも新たに誕生した。旅館であることを忘れてはいけないという先代の思いを受け、次世代につないでいくための真髄の結晶でもある。信楽焼きの陶器風呂や和風な玄関、じゅうたんなど随所に日本の伝統を感じさせる工夫をしている。押しつけがましくなく自然な流れの中で謙虚に表現している。昔、日本家屋でおもてなしをされているような、古き良き日本人のDNAを呼び起こさせる感じがする。百余年という悠久の流れを受け止め、次世代にお客さまとともにつないでいく。常にお客さまと向き合う真摯な姿勢をいつまでも…という願いを本書に託した。

株式会社オータパブリケイションズ　執行役員　山下裕乃

98

館 お茶の水

AN OCHANOMIZU HO

ホテル龍名
HOTEL RYUMEI

龍名館、時を越える
ホテル龍名館お茶の水本店

2015年6月30日　第1刷発行

著者	株式会社龍名館
発行者	太田進
発行所	株式会社オータパブリケイションズ
	〒105-0001　東京都港区虎ノ門1-19-5虎ノ門1丁目森ビル
	電話　03-5251-9800
	info@ohtapub.co.jp
印刷・製本	富士美術印刷株式会社
Book Design	株式会社Z
Translation	株式会社トランス・アジア
Photographer	金本広章／株式会社木下写場
	藤林慶海知／株式会社マリーマーブル
	逸見幸生／新田健二

©Ryumeikan 2015 printed in Japan
乱丁・落丁は小社にてお取り換えいたします。
ISBN978-4-903721-52-1　C0052　定価はカバーに表示してあります。

＜禁無断転訳載＞
本書の一部または複写・複製・転訳載・磁気媒体・CD-ROMへの入力を禁じます。
これらの承諾については、TEL03-5251-9800までご照会ください。